LEADERSHIP
A Leadership Fable
RESIDUE

GALEN D. BINGHAM

Copyright © 2015 Leadership Residue, LLC.
All rights reserved.

ISBN: 1505361508
ISBN 13: 9781505361506
Library of Congress Control Number: 2014921736
CreateSpace Independent Publishing Platform
North Charleston, South Carolina

Acknowledgments:
THANK YOU, THANK YOU, THANK YOU

The roots of this book stem from observing the impact leaders have had in my life and professional career. Friends, mentors, and heroes have fanned a passion that has resulted in the book you now hold. Joe Cavaliere and Stan Hutchen are constantly in the back of my mind as I think of how to lead others. Kelvin Taylor, Bill Ellis, and Derek Mays encouraged me to put structure around an idea birthed on a golf course. Lisa Fey, K. P. Westmoreland, Shep Hyken, and Karin Hurt opened doors to the idea that leadership development could be more than a passing interest. Heather Luby and other writers helped me understand the art and business of writing. Ron Moore, Carl Kwapong, and Roy Jackson encouraged me to seize an opportunity for greatness versus settling for being just as good as others. Thank you to Gary Brooks, whose inspirational book is forthcoming, for providing my first forum to share my passion for leadership publicly. I am eternally grateful to all who contributed their personal stories of leadership residue. Their friendship, transparency, and commitment to this project have fueled a movement.

Finally, thank you to George and Sherlean Bingham, who, as parents, encourage me to live in the knowledge of ancestors whose experiences obligate me to aspire for greatness. I thank Regis Bingham and Dana Bingham-Guanilo, whose support have been unwavering. My daughter, Landis Bingham, taught me to think of dreams like baking bread: "If you keep them in the oven too long, they might burn." To my wife and life mate, Monique Garris-Bingham, I am grateful for her love and continued encouragement to pursue what inspires me to help others.

CONTENTS

Preface: Grandma's Coconut Pound Cake ix

Part 1: Business as Usual 1
The Opportunity 3
The Final Dry Run 7
New Problems with Clone 11
Dorothy Reflects in Her Office 14

Part 2: Tornado Ensues. 17
The Daydream 19
The Exam 34
The Morning After 36
The Ultimatum 42
The Alternative 44

Part 3: Moment of Truth 49
Clarity 51
Meeting with Jeremy 56
Proposal at BO Corp 61
The Response 66

Part 4: New Beginnings **69**
Months Later 71
The Grind. 74
Lessons from the Journey 78

Part 5: Tools and Resources **95**
Dorothy's Submission 97
Professor Wicco's Assigned Reading List 99
Crafting Dorothy's Leadership Platform 101
Crafting Dorothy's Leadership Residue Plan 102

Part 6: Real Life Examples of Leadership Residue **103**
No Fiction Here 105

Part 7: Notes from the Author **123**
My Leadership Residue Story: 125
My Leadership Platform: Building Bridges, Solving Problems,
and Leading Authentically 127

Epilogue: Here's the Point **129**

Beans Wall Quote #145: "Each of us influences at least ten thousand people during our lifetime. The question is not whether but how you use your influence." — John Maxwell

Preface:
GRANDMA'S COCONUT POUND CAKE

Educators, ministers, friends, and family felt the vibration of wooden planks as they crossed the only bridge leading into a small riverboat town on the Mississippi Delta. All were traveling a familiar road to attend a home-going celebration. Willie Mae Gaddy lived to be eighty-six years old.

In May 2007, countless stories told of visiting my grandma in a sleepy Civil War town called Helena—West Helena, Arkansas. Everyone reminisced about leaving "fat-cat full" and with smiles equally wide on their faces. Grandma Gaddy once said, "We can't give you a lot of money, but we can make sure the memory of your meals in this house will carry you through the short-money times."

It was true. As tough as times might get, just thinking about Grandma's kitchen could transport everyone to happier times—times laced with tastes and aromas of sweet-potato pie, pecan pie, thirty-day friendship cake, and German chocolate cake. The flavors came back to life as vividly as if floating from her kitchen.

Lean in, and you just might be able to smell the hint of vanilla and cinnamon coming through these very pages. It was never difficult to guess what treat would emerge next from my grandma's kitchen. My nose could solve every mystery. Her legacy remains well after she has gone. What a wonderful legacy to leave for friends, family, and strangers to remember.

What if leaders could conjure the same sense of legacy? We have all been called *leader*. Whether due to a formal title, circumstances calling on unique expertise, or tenure, at some point everyone has felt the weight of leadership.

Most take on the role with reverence, understanding the responsibility associated with the label. If you are like me, you've worked late hours and compromised family commitments, adopting the burdens of others as if they were your own. Have you ever stopped to wonder if your extra effort really matters?

Think about it for a moment. We all work hard. Most of us, with any fortune, will move on to more important responsibilities. Direct reports will move on. Will it have mattered that you were the leader instead of someone else? Did your late hours really make a difference in the long run? Will your leadership inspire others even when you are no longer around? Or will you be replaced in the hearts and minds of your followers as easily as someone typing a new organizational chart?

If you deem yourself an effective leader, I hope this book will encourage you to keep going even when no one is aware of your efforts. I hope this book will persuade you to use a longer lens to evaluate how others experience your leadership. I hope to show you how lessons learned under your leadership can be remembered as fondly as my grandma's famous coconut pound cake, which was my personal favorite.

This book is not about management tactics that promise seven keys to superior leadership, five steps for ensuring accountability, or methods for learning how to walk and talk with leadership authority. Instead I will attempt to encourage all leaders, but people leaders in particular, to embrace three primary responsibilities:

1. Paint a clear picture of success.
2. Inspire action.
3. Remove barriers.

Leadership residue encompasses the inspiration that remains, sustains, and influences behavior even when the leader is no longer physically around. Residue can be positive and negative; in both instances, it transcends formal reporting structures.

Positive residue is like a brilliant rainbow after a cool spring shower or the feeling you have after watching a favorite movie. This leadership empowers the best in all of us. It inspires followers to see themselves as part owners in the success of the task or mission.

Positive residue compels followers to invest their discretionary time, creative insights, and valued personal resources to ensure success. Not only does the leader receive what is requested, but in addition followers look to overcome unanticipated obstacles. The internal reward of knowing the mission is accomplished at the highest possible standard is as valuable as the compensation paid for doing the work.

Negative residue is just the opposite. It is a prompt of the worst of times. Like the memory of a sad life event, it can leave people feeling drained, deflated, and willing to contribute only the bare minimum needed to complete the task.

With negative residue, followers feel as empowered as a cog in a wheel. Instead of taking ownership, they view work as just a job. Value is defined by the size of the paycheck alone. Allegiance to the vision is rented at best and evaporates into thin air when a better-paying opportunity appears.

One's residue is a proof point of his or her effectiveness as a leader. It ensures the sustainability of any mission. It powers the engine of realizing the leader's vision and is therefore too important to leave to chance.

The aim of this book is to encourage and empower leaders to be purposeful in attempting to positively affect those who follow. The benefits of leaving a positive residue are long lasting and will inspire others to want to become leaders themselves.

In the end, people long to be inspired. They want to be freed to do their best work. They want to benefit the organization for which they work sometimes fifty or sixty hours each week. Many want to do meaningful work; others want to see just how good they can be.

Based on my experience, I am convinced every major success and failure begins and ends with leadership—plain and simple. There is a necessary role for managing short-term tasks; without short-term successes there can be no endurance for long-term victory. Leadership, however, is much more inspirational than management and should not be evaluated by short-term management metrics. A necessary measure of leadership, therefore, is the influence that remains after the leader has gone. As you will see in the following pages, a leader's residue can be as vivid to followers as memories of my grandma's coconut pound cake are to me.

You can join this global leadership conversation through the following social-media sites:

Facebook: https://www.facebook.com/LeadersResidue
Twitter: https://twitter.com/LeadersResidue
Blog: https://leadershipresidue.wordpress.com
Website: www.Leadership-Residue.com.

Now I would like to tell you a story.

PART 1
BUSINESS AS USUAL

Beans Wall Quote #147. "A boss creates fear, a leader confidence. A boss fixes blame, a leader corrects mistakes. A boss knows, a leader asks questions." — Russell H. Ewing

THE OPPORTUNITY

A faint afternoon chill slipped through the opened window of Dorothy's corner office at WB Tech Solutions (Whizz Bang Technological Solutions). It was common to have an office full of windows on the fifth floor. Many of the leased office buildings charged top dollar for views of the bay. It was rare, however, to have windows open to a breeze—a comfort Dorothy insisted upon before signing the lease.

It wasn't Dorothy's money, but she would be the one coming in early, staying late, and working weekends. She negotiated the additional creature comfort. Dorothy rarely lost a negotiation when she knew what she wanted. A breeze from the bay was no exception.

Over the years, many had been disarmed by Dorothy's petite frame. Her faint-brown freckles and auburn curls frequently caused problems with getting her into bars and nightclubs in her youth. Fortunately, Dorothy drank only occasionally, and she hadn't been to a nightclub in over ten years. Dorothy dedicated every moment of time and every ounce of energy to achieving her two career goals: becoming CEO of a Fortune 500 firm and becoming filthy rich.

At the age of thirty-four, Dorothy had already logged more office hours than others at her firm twenty years her senior. It was a work ethic she attributed to having grown up on her aunt's farm in Kansas. Others saw her as tireless, driven—almost manic.

Tessie tapped lightly at the door three times. Her sleepy Georgia accent seemed to float over the quiet of the room. She leaned only her head in the doorway. "Ms. Dorothy, conference room B is all set up for you."

Tessie had come to Dorothy through a temp agency. She was working as an administrative assistant while trying to fund courses at LCC (Local Community College). Although older than Dorothy, Tessie admired her boss for being a woman in a male-dominated industry. Tessie saw Dorothy as a model of what a woman could achieve with a good education, a strong work ethic, and a take-no-prisoners approach.

Dorothy looked up from the computer screen, smiling warmly at Tessie. Using a single finger, Dorothy adjusted the black-framed glasses that frequently slipped down her nose. Using her middle finger to make the adjustment was a habit even Catholic school nuns of her youth couldn't break, though many tried. Most of the time, her habit was innocent and unconscious. Other times, Dorothy leveraged her widely known idiosyncrasy to send hard-to-miss messages of contempt. The distinction lay in the piercing stare occasionally lingering behind the adjustment.

Dorothy responded in a polite tone easily mistakable for a compliment. "Now, Tessie Mae, did you just say 'conference room B'? I remember being quite clear. I need the A conference room. Unless conference room A has caught on fire or is under biological quarantine, I expect to see it set up in less than five minutes. Not B—A."

With a bubbly demeanor common among southern women, Tessie responded as if sharing the key to a mysterious riddle. "Oh! You meant *conference room A*. When you said, 'Set up A conference room,' I thought you meant pick any conference room. I picked conference room B because I like the warm colors and how the light bounces off the table. I didn't know you meant *conference room A* specifically. Ain't it funny how the two phrases sound similar but have different meanings?"

Dorothy readjusted her glasses without taking her eyes off of Tessie and smiled. "*Ain't* it funny?" This time, Dorothy's smile chilled and lingered a bit longer than before.

As senior vice president of WB Tech, Dorothy had done everything she could think of to prepare for the next day's business meeting. This presentation alone could allow her to bypass the CEO part of her career goal and go straight to filthy rich.

LEADERSHIP RESIDUE

Dorothy's and WB Tech's financial dreams hinged on a holographic technology developed under the technical code name CL053. With advancements in high-definition three-dimensional television, CL053 could transport a picture-perfect holographic image around the world. It was the type of technological breakthrough allowing twenty-nine-year-old Silicon Valley whiz kids to retire to the Cayman Islands.

Jeremy was this particular whiz kid. Born and raised in New Jersey, he had begun tinkering with computers when he was eight years old, building gaming systems, robots, and software applications. While other preadolescents learned the Boy Scout motto, the art of trading hockey cards, or the beauty of turning a double play on the sandlot with friends, Jeremy learned advanced computer animation. When he was a child, his parents encouraged him socially. They said he needed to learn how to make friends. They even applied for his admittance to Mensa International three times so he could at least meet other übersmart children. Jeremy wanted nothing to do with Mensa or with the idea of making friends. By chance or by calculation, he managed to score in the ninety-fifth percentile in the Mensa admittance exams, missing the cutoff by exactly three points each time. So Jeremy kept to himself, tinkering with computers until he was old enough to move out of his parents' house.

Eleven years later, Jeremy was the talk of the tech world. CL053 had been featured in technology magazines and was the hit at every party for the superrich crowd. With a three-dimensional high-definition television and the CL053 transmitter, one item could be in two places at the same time. Jeremy was a technological genius. Unfortunately, he lacked the business knowledge and social skills needed to build commercial success. Jeremy hired Dorothy to turn his creation into more than a mere high-tech novelty.

Dorothy's background, passion, and vision solidified her as the perfect choice for Jeremy and WB Tech. Dorothy's charge was to bring CL053 into the mainstream market and prove its value as a billion-dollar brand.

Venture capitalists and savvy tech companies look for up-and-coming technology to acquire. It was reasonable to assume Google or Microsoft might be interested in CL053 once it became a member of the billion-dollar club. A product doesn't have to make a billion dollars; it merely has to demonstrate a plausible likelihood that it will. If Dorothy could be part of leading this success, she would be on the short list for occupying the corner office of every technology start-up in the industry. Or, if she chose, she could cash in stock options at the age of thirty-five and never work again.

Dorothy sacrificed dating, starting a family, and socializing with friends to succeed. It was Dorothy's idea to create a brand name more identifiable by the general public. Clone tested well in focus groups. Many felt it legitimized a technology many people believed would exist only in *The Jetsons* cartoons or *Star Trek* reruns. Dorothy set out to develop a niche in the business-teleconference industry. She even developed a tag line to educate consumers about the brand and suggest a need in the current business environment. *Why subject critical meetings to the limitations of voice and video conferencing? When you can't be there in person, send a Clone.*

THE FINAL DRY RUN

Dorothy left nothing to chance. She needed tomorrow to be perfect. She double-checked calculations and reviewed product attributes. Having rehearsed the presentation seven times over the past three days, she knew every word and could address any potential question from the audience of corporate executives. Today was the final dry run of Clone with her team of senior technology managers. Dorothy's desk intercom beeped, and Tessie announced conference room A was set up. Everyone but Branson was on the line.

BO Corp (Big Opportunity Corporation) was by far the largest business opportunity coming their way. The scale of this opportunity wasn't lost on anyone, least of all Dorothy. Three weeks before, Dorothy had sent her four top engineers to BO Corp's key cities. Although headquartered in Seattle, Washington, they were expanding globally at a rapid pace. Today, Dorothy's team called in from four corners of the world. Sue was in Santiago, Chile. Matt called from Monterey, Mexico. Larsen chimed in from London, England, and Branson was in Shanghai, China. Today would be the final test of the demonstration occurring the following day.

"Where is Branson?" Dorothy inquired without lifting her eyes from the computer screen.

"Oh, he texted he's held up in traffic. He'll be online in just a few. Will that do, hon?" Tessie's southern disposition seemed to make even the largest inconvenience a little more pleasant. However, even Tessie couldn't ease Dorothy's tension today.

"I suppose that will have to *do*, won't it?" Sarcasm was an art Dorothy had practiced since college. It was yet another tool she used to communicate disapproval.

Dorothy made her way to conference room A. Everything was in place. With the click of a button, three of Dorothy's four colleagues appeared on individual television monitors positioned in the conference room. More important, Dorothy's picture-perfect hologram appeared in three corners of the planet.

The technology worked perfectly yet again. The face on Dorothy's Clone lit up as she received applause from her colleagues. The projection was perfect. They could see every crinkle in Dorothy's smile, every freckle on her cheek, and every twist of her curls. Dorothy calmed the applause by waving her hands as if wanting to make an announcement.

"Guys, I know this has been a long journey. You worked on this even before I came to WB Tech. All you needed was leadership, vision, and business savvy to pull this all together. My success tomorrow will validate all of your long hours and dedication. I know I'm not easy to please at times."

The faces on screens nodded in agreement.

Dorothy paced the floor as she continued. "Some say it's my nature to accept nothing but the best. It'll be my focus, tenacity, and commitment to winning that'll bring this home. Unfortunately, none of you will be in the room when I present the fruit of your labor. Wowing the audiences is what I do best. All I need is good material to work with. You can all sleep well tonight. I've got it from here."

Transmitter cameras followed Dorothy as she walked to an ice bucket at the end of the conference table. She picked up a bottle of champagne chilled in ice and brought it into view of the transmitter.

"Larsen, can you read the label on the bottle?" Dorothy held the bottle with both hands as a waiter might present a wine selection to a discerning guest.

Larsen leaned forward to look at the holographic image. "Dom Pérignon, 1963."

"That's right. Nothing but the best as I toast to our success." With those words, Dorothy poured the sixty-dollar-a-glass champagne into a long-stemmed glass. Midpour, the Shanghai monitor popped on as Branson sat at his seat.

Branson fluffed his hair and flashed a nervous smile as he attempted to join the conversation. "I see you guys didn't wait for me. What did I miss?"

"So glad you could join us, Branson. Tessie said you may have decided to take a vacation day to take in the sights of Shanghai." Dorothy turned slowly on her heels. A glare from Dorothy's hologram had the same effect as if she were physically in the conference room.

Larsen volunteered to bring his teammate up to speed. "You didn't miss much, B. Our fearless leader there in the emerald city of Seattle was reminding us old farts just how lucky we are to have her."

Everyone looked at Dorothy. Her face broke into a smile, choking a little as she sipped at her champagne. All four screens joined in the subdued laughter.

Dorothy looked at Larsen and adjusted her glasses. "OK, guys, let's get to work. I want to check a few RI readings while we're all together." She moved to a laptop at the end of the table. "On my end, I see—"

"What is that?" Matt's outburst interrupted Dorothy.

"Come on, Matt, enough playing around. I need your reality-image reading." Dorothy never veered her focus from her laptop.

Matt hurriedly typed on his keyboard. "I know what RI readings are; that's not what I mean."

"You mean it wasn't just me? It happened here too!" murmured Larsen.

Dorothy looked up to see Matt's and Larsen's frantic faces. "Guys, what's going on? Your career is on the line if I find out this is some kind of practical joke."

Sue had been quiet for most of the call. Now her face on the Santiago monitor was almost gray. "Guys, I think we have a problem." Sue flipped through manuals and typed frantically before continuing. "It's gone."

The look on Dorothy's face left little room for interpretation. She wanted answers. "What's gone? You guys aren't making any sense. What are your RI readings?"

Matt stopped typing and looked intensely at his computer screen. "Zero," he said, looking directly at the camera.

Larsen also stopped typing also. "My RI rating is zero as well."

Sue had yet to blink. Her face lost even more color. "I was wrong; we don't have a problem. We have a *big* problem."

Dorothy was visibly beside herself with frustration. "What do you mean, zero? Zero is impossible, guys. There has to be some value to the reading. A zero would mean..." Dorothy stopped midsentence, speechless.

Branson had been quiet since joining the conference. His face suggested he had no idea what was happening. He broke the quiet that had begun to hum across the airways. "Of course the RI is zero. We haven't started the hologram transmission yet. I've been watching the four of you on video chat since I walked in. When are we going to start the show?"

Larson, Matt, Sue, and now Dorothy remained silent.

NEW PROBLEMS WITH CLONE

"I want answers, and I want them *now!*" Dorothy's tirades occurred more frequently since she had advanced to senior levels in her career. She took pride in delivering results. Hers was a track record not to be compromised by anything or anyone.

Sue was the most experienced of the team of engineers. "Well, it's obvious something happened to the holograph right at the time Branson came online."

Dorothy assumed a calm tone, which did nothing to calm the situation. "Is *something* a catchy phrase you fifty-year-old kids use instead of saying 'I don't know'? Can one of you tell me what you *do* know?"

Branson spoke up. "Hey, I'm only forty-eight, and I just got here, so leave me out of this."

Larsen reminded everyone the hologram had worked perfectly in the beginning. "This was the best I'd ever seen. I checked when we started, and I had an RI of four hundred thirty-eight, a full thirty-seven points better than anything I've seen."

Matt perked up. "No, I think Sue is on to something. Everything was perfect on my end as well. I didn't check RI, but it had to be in the mid–four hundreds. Everything changed when Branson joined the session."

"Hey, you guys aren't blaming me for this. All I did was sit down and boot up the system." Branson's voice wobbled with concern.

Sue continued, "No, Branson, no one's saying you did anything wrong. Think about it. We've always been online when Dorothy initiated past sessions. We've never tested what would happen if someone joined a session already in progress. This could be a real breakthrough."

"Breakthrough? Did you just say *breakthrough?*" Dorothy didn't appear amused by the discussion. "Are you saying the four of you have been working on this project for years, and you just stumbled upon a new problem? A problem of this magnitude will take weeks to validate, let alone fix. We paid to fly the four of you to all parts of the world, taught you new technology, and overpaid your salaries for you to happen upon the possibility you may need to test for something as simple as—I don't know—someone joining a session already in progress! Tell me this is a practical joke. I'll fire only one of you for instigating a practical joke when I'm under such pressure trying to save this company. Call this a practical joke, I fire one of you, and the rest of us go on to make tons of money. But the level of incompetence you are proposing here would get all of you fired."

Dorothy continued after a small but tension filled pause. "Fortunately for you, I'm under the gun right now trying to save this company. I'll make a deal with you. All of you can keep your jobs if, in the next four hours, you are able to validate the problem and chart a path to fix it. In four hours, I want an e-mail from one of you detailing what you'd like me to say to Jeremy about your lapse in basic job responsibility."

They all looked at their watches as Dorothy continued. "By eight in the morning PST, I want another e-mail indicating the problem is fixed. I don't want to hear you're working on it, it's almost fixed, or you need to make a few minor adjustments. Fixed! I've worked too hard to save this company for my career to be ruined because a few underworked and overpaid engineers were more concerned about their AARP discount at the local zoo than doing their jobs. Last I checked, there's not much of a job market for fifty-year-old computer engineers who failed on their last assignment."

Everyone looked shell-shocked. Prior to ending what had become a high-definition video chat, Dorothy unleashed an insult she had honed since college. "I've seen this circus before. I warn you, your high-wire act has no net." Just before she signed off, she adjusted her glasses one last time with her trademark lingering stare and uttered one more comment: "Branson, if you are ever running late to another meeting, keep driving to the unemployment office."

Perhaps Dorothy's recent explosion was an example of why the team had taken to calling her **WBW** *(Wicked Bitch of the West)* behind her back.

DOROTHY REFLECTS IN HER OFFICE

To say Dorothy was upset would be to call the problem with the *Titanic* a slight miscalculation. Tessie was the only person around to hear her rant as she passed through the lobby on her way to her office.

"I can't believe the incompetence…This is what I have to work with…If it weren't for me, they wouldn't have even tested the system…All of this the night before the biggest proposal of my career…I won't damage my reputation for them…If I'm going down, *everybody's* going down!"

After Dorothy had calmed slightly, Tessie's voice came over the intercom. "Ma'am, I have a few messages for you. Would you like them now, or do you need a few more minutes?"

"No, now is fine." Dorothy's voice conveyed the exhaustion of the evening.

Tessie came in, cheery as ever. She brought with her a handful of yellow sticky notes and a pot of coffee. The aroma filled the office as Tessie walked toward a small wooden table near Dorothy's desk. Dorothy flipped through the messages as Tessie poured a cup of coffee.

- *"Jeremy to arrive late. Will meet you for coffee tomorrow morning."*
- *"BO Corp meeting confirmed for eleven o'clock in the morning."*
- *"AU (Anywhere University) called for contribution to alumni fund."*

LEADERSHIP RESIDUE 15

Dorothy paused to consider each note. The last one softened her eyes and brought a faint upturn to the corners of her lips. Note in hand, she turned toward the window, pausing to gaze at the bay.

"Thanks, Tess. Hey, that smells good." Dorothy temporarily snapped from her trance.

Tessie's smile grew. "Thanks. I don't drink a lot of coffee myself, but don't you just love the aroma? Sometimes I brew coffee just to fill the room. It's totally different from the coffee from the grocery store. I tried all of them, ya know—all of the grocery store brands, that is. It must be something about the beans they use."

Dorothy sipped her coffee. "Something about the beans?"

"Yeah, the only difference I can think of is the beans," Tessie replied.

Dorothy sipped again from her cup as she turned to gaze once more at the bay through the window. "It's funny—I haven't heard that phrase since college."

"Yeah?" Tessie paused to collect envelopes that had collected in the out box on Dorothy's desk.

Dorothy continued gazing through the window and stirred her coffee. "Actually it was the advertising slogan for a coffee shop where a lot of us studied."

Tessie stood at the edge of Dorothy's desk and looked on with admiring eyes for fifteen seconds before speaking. "Ms. Dorothy, I just want you to know I admire everything you're doing. I guess those old-timers just ain't used to spitfires like us—I mean, you—being in charge and all. I talk about you all the time to my classmates at LCC. This company is doing some awesome work. I don't understand all of it. Truth is I don't understand any of it, but it sounds important. Without you showing them what's what, I can tell this company just wouldn't be the same."

Tessie continued as she walked closer to Dorothy's desk. "When I graduate next year, I'm going on to a university just like you. Before long I'll be wearing fancy suits, ordering people around, and making silver-haired men shake when I come in the room just like—I mean, I wouldn't be called those names behind my—well, you know. At the risk of sounding unprofessional, I just want you to know you are quite the inspiration to me."

Tessie headed toward the door. She looked back as she opened it. Dorothy smiled and thanked her for the cup of coffee and mini pep talk. Turning back to the window, Dorothy whispered to herself, "Great. Now I've got a groupie working for me."

Dorothy looked deeper into the bay and whispered to herself again as she sipped at her coffee. "I'm not sure how much I admire me at this moment."

The window casted a reflection of Dorothy's office. She noticed the stack of telephone messages Tessie had delivered earlier. The top message was from her alma mater. Her time at AU seemed a hundred years ago but in fact had only been fifteen.

"The business world seemed so simple when I was on the outside looking in," she said to herself.

As a half smile softened the corners of her mouth, Dorothy picked up the notes. In a moment of inspiration, she walked to the bookshelf and searched the only shelf containing something other than technical trade magazines and operating manuals.

Behind the glass plaques and President's Club awards sat a lone photograph in a faux wooden frame. The picture was of Dorothy and three friends from college outside of their favorite college hangout, a coffee shop called Beans.

"We certainly thought we had all of the answers. We couldn't wait to change the world. If only life was as clear today as we made it out to be. Back then, the most pressing issue was earning a good grade on an assignment. I busted my ass in college only so I could fail the biggest examination of my career in the morning."

Dorothy paused and then took the photo back to her desk. Gazing through the window, she allowed herself to be transported fifteen years in the past to college days with friends. Images and memories were as vivid as if they had occurred only fifteen minutes ago.

PART 2
TORNADO ENSUES

Beans Wall Quote #193: "Courage is fear holding on a minute longer"—General George S. Patton

THE DAYDREAM

It was nine o'clock, and the sun had begun giving up on Dorothy three hours ago. This was her fifth straight hour of studying, and it promised not to be the last for the evening. Finals week was a rite of passage that escaped no one at AU. The tension was as thick as government-issued peanut butter. Previous students had rubbed the dorm-room furniture worn over the years. Etching once passing for wood grain no longer convinced anyone.

"It's obvious this isn't wood. Would it kill the dean to spend some of my tuition money on real wooden furniture?" Dorothy talked aloud to dust bunnies peeking at her from the corner. Big-can grocery-store coffee did little to calm her nerves. But it was all a college student could afford, especially a student from small-town Kansas.

As an AU senior, Dorothy worked hard to distinguish herself. She had a strong grade-point average and was captain or president of almost every business-related student organization on campus. None of her accolades gave her confidence she would score well on the final exam for Organizational Leadership 415. She and her friends always seemed to miss the mark when it came to anticipating Dr. Wicco.

Professor Wilson Wicco led Organizational Leadership 415. As a capstone course, his class could determine cumulative grade-point averages and class rankings. He bragged about former students who had gone on to prestigious MBA programs. Many led major business corporations or nonprofit organizations. He was tough and demanded a lot. During the first day of class, he described his calling as to "weed out students who would not make it in the real world." He said he provided a public service to businesses and graduate programs, which, in his opinion, "put too much value in touchy-feely accomplishments, which do not predict future success against real-world assignments or tasks in business."

Required reading consisted of many of the best-read business and leadership books of our time: *Good to Great, Fierce Conversations, Change the World,* and *The Five Dysfunctions of a Team,* just to name a few. After requiring almost complete memorization of key passages, Wicco was known to spend entire class periods espousing his personal views as to where he believed these authors had gone astray. Students complained they could never tell if their work should reflect ideas from the reading or notes captured during one of Wicco's classroom rants.

With no midcourse assignments, grades were based entirely on an in-class essay to be completed on the final day of class. Wicco would award As to the top 5 percent of all scorers. He would also add glowing letters of endorsement in those students' permanent records along with access to his personal network of friends and alumni. Students scoring below the top 5 percent were awarded grades on a scale ranging from C to F. He said this grading scale better reflected assessments in the world after college.

Many of his frequent classroom pontifications would end with "contrary to how your mommies have programmed you little munchkins, in the real world, you are either exceptional or average." Behind his back, students called him Wicked Wicco. His reputation and classroom antics persuaded Dorothy to join the congregation of believers.

Now Dorothy was preparing to face the largest exam of her college career. Success on this examination could open doors to a future she could barely imagine. Still, she and her friends would have no way of knowing how to prepare.

Dorothy received a video-chat request at 8:00 p.m. "What up, what up, what up!" Unannounced, Louis's voice boomed through her laptop speakers.

Most people greeted by saying hello; Louis always announced his entrance with a roar. Somehow he had figured out how to turn off the discreet—and much more civilized—ping announcing all other chat requests.

As unsettling as a Louis greeting is in public, try receiving one while alone in a dorm room, Dorothy thought as she dabbed up a coffee spill caused by Louis.

Louis was enrolled in Wilson Wicco's Organizational Leadership 415 class as well, as were a few more of Dorothy's friends.

"Rather than burning the midnight oil by yourself, why don't you join us?" he asked. "Jack, Tim, and I are studying together at Beans. We persuaded Ozzie to play Miles Davis all night to help us prepare for Wicked Wicco. If we're going to fail, we might as well enjoy good coffee and Miles in the process. Besides, this could be our last chance to hang out together."

Dorothy tried to squeeze a word in the conversation to explain now wasn't the time. "I need to finish my second reread of Dr. Wicco's case against *Start With Why* by Simon Sinek...and I need some alone time too...and I haven't been sleeping well...and I need to focus so I can—"

Louis cut her off with his trademark roar. "D-D-D-D-Dee, I told you the gang is all here, and Ozzie is playing Miles. You might buy into Wacko's nonsense about not needing friends in the real world. But you aren't in the corner office yet, and we're your friends, at least until you ditch us at graduation. By royal decree of *the Gang*, you are ordered to be here! I'm out!" As abruptly as the chat began, it ended, and Louis was gone.

Dorothy thought perhaps Louis was right. It would be good to have one last study marathon. She had fond memories of pulling all-nighters with her friends. She absolutely adored the muted trumpet of Miles Davis. Even his miscues seemed to clear any lingering concerns. For Dorothy, Miles Davis was like a beautiful tornado blowing across Kansas plains.

So she packed up her laptop, threw an armful of books into her backpack, and jumped in her car. Dorothy owned a ten-year-old Toyota Tercel. She called her car Toto because it had been like a good friend throughout her time at AU. The last two letters had fallen off the Toyota emblem on the back of her car, so it only read *TOYO*—practically the same as its nickname. She had paid $250 for it three years ago and spent $500 in maintenance each year to keep it running. Toto always took her where she needed to go and brought her back safely. Other students drove nicer, more expensive cars paid for by their parents. Although the car was ten years old, Dorothy loved the feeling of independence she felt when traveling with Toto.

Toto came through again, and Dorothy arrived to find her friends at their usual table. The aroma of coffee filled the shop, and Miles Davis was doing his best to soothe their concerns.

"Look who's here!" Tim yelled from across the room.

For Tim, two plus two always equaled four. There were right and wrong answers to every problem. He was an AU triple legacy. He would be the third generation in a family of chemical engineers. He would be the third generation in his family to graduate in the top 10 percent of his class at AU. Still, earning a scholarship to his first-choice graduate school always seemed to be a topic of conversation for Tim. For as long as his friends had known him, he had talked about a life plan hinged on a graduate degree from EWU (Everyone Wants-you University). Having the grades and GRE scores to gain acceptance was never in question. Tim had transferred to AU from the prestigious SPU (Smart People University) at the beginning of junior year. It surprised no one when he enrolled in Organizational Leadership 415 because of Dr. Wicco's connections to EWU. A number of Wicco's students went on to be alumnus of EWU. A few were currently senior faculty there as well. A well-placed letter of endorsement coupled with strong academic credentials could go a long way toward securing Tim's full scholarship.

"So, Dorothy finally decided to show up with her precious Toto. When are you going to shoot your dog of a car and buy some *real* transportation, one with a fuel efficiency rating—*any* fuel efficiency rating?" Tim's wit cut to the core of every matter. Although typically grounded in truth, he seldom showed sensitivity.

Jack came to Dorothy's defense. "Tim, would you stop teasing?"

Jack had a good heart but was perceived as a bit Pollyanna in his view of the world. He was often found wearing something with a peace symbol or the phrase *"life is good"* on it. Jack was quick to support the cause du jour if it offered a possibility to help create a better life for the less fortunate. Jack said he had enrolled in Organizational Leadership 415 because after graduating he wanted to help people. What better way to help people than as their servant leader?

Unfortunately Jack spent so much time supporting causes there was often not enough time for studying. His grades suffered because of it—so much so this was Jack's third year as a senior. Because of the three weeks he had spent supporting the Student Alliance's protest against poor-quality campus food, he was again in danger of not graduating. Nothing less than an A in Organizational Leadership 415 would ensure his graduating this year.

"We all know Dorothy is doing the best she can," Jack continued. "Toto is obviously much more than just a car to Dorothy. Good friends cannot be easily replaced. If you had a heart, you just might understand."

"Cut the crap, both of you." Louis was a former AU middle linebacker. AU wasn't the type of school to produce NFL prospects. There was talk in the athletic department of Louis being the first. At six feet three inches and weighing 238 pounds, Louis could bench-press 252 pounds forty-three times without a break. He could also run a forty-yard sprint in 4.21 seconds. Those were statistics any NFL hopeful would love to claim.

Coming off Louis's strong sophomore season, the coaching staff had added three top high school recruits. AU was the preseason pick to win the conference the following year. As teams prepared to play AU, "containing Louis" was the highlight of every competitive scouting report.

Playing in the third conference game of his junior year, Louis had shattered his left knee. AU had supported his reconstructive surgery and full rehabilitation. He was off crutches and participating in light workouts before the end of the season. Doctors warned a good hit could cause permanent damage. Louis defied warnings and returned to the field his senior year, but he was never again the dominating force that his team and NFL scouts had known.

Louis rallied his classmates. "We're here for one reason: to bring Dr. Weirdo to his knees. I heard last year's students left his final exam in tears. When we're done with Professor Weak-o, he's going to be the one bawling like a baby."

Beans was a popular meeting place just off campus. There was free Wi-Fi, good coffee, plenty of space to spread out, and real wooden tables. Ozzie was the shop owner. His gray hair elicited frequent comparisons to Sean Connery. He had an extensive music collection, which he would play as a backdrop to enhance the customer experience. Rumor had it he had bought Beans fifteen years before, after a successful career as a partner with a top global consulting firm. He seemed to have an endless supply of obscure leadership and motivational quotations—some from famous leaders and noted authors, others seemingly from his own life experiences. Hundreds of numbered quote placards decorated the coffee-shop walls. Students took pride in memorizing Beans's wall quotes, reference numbers and all.

Ozzie and Beans were legendary among students and alumni alike. Somehow everyone felt smarter when they were there. Some credited the shop's success to its Colombian coffee blends, rare wall art, and extensive music collection. Others said Beans's success was the product of well-honed business acumen. Everyone called Ozzie a wizard for creating a culture and experience. He frequently drew attention from national publications wanting interviews, all of which he rejected.

There were numerous offers to help Ozzie expand, franchise, or sell. Some wanted to make him the next Howard Schultz. Ozzie always chuckled at the notion of creating the next Starbucks. He said he was content with being the owner of a college coffee shop. When asked about the secrets to his success, he would flash a boyish grin and repeat his advertising slogan—"It's all about the Beans." Amid the hype, one could sense Ozzie was comfortable in his skin and happy with his life.

Dorothy and her friends would need all the wisdom they could find. Ozzie recognized the looks on the faces of his loyal customers.

"The looks of desperation lead me to believe Organizational Leadership 415 is somehow involved. It must be time for Wicco's final examination. When will Wilson learn from Dwight D. Eisenhower—'You don't lead by hitting people over the head; that's assault, not leadership'?" Everyone nodded in agreement. He added, "Let me know about this pot of Colombia dark roast. I'll visit the grower next week."

The gang pored over the books piled on a table in the back of the shop. They sipped cups of dark roast and turned up the table speaker just as Miles began the swirling interlude to "Sketches of Spain." There were five large tables in the back of Beans. The space was perfect for friends gathering to play board games, study while listening to music, or just enjoy great coffee. The atmosphere of the place had become legendary. Although the music was selected at the front counter, every large table had a speaker, which allowed for individual volume adjustment. The sound of music reverberating from so many places created an acoustical paradise.

Louis interrupted Miles with an outburst. "We need to beat the bastard with his own stick!" Dorothy flinched and looked at him in horror, but he continued, "Wacko, beat Professor Wacko to the punch—you know, anticipate everything he might throw at us. I say we do tonight like one of his crazy classes. Who's down for a little mud wrestling with Dr. Wacolicious?"

Everyone despised Wicco's class. No matter how much they studied, he would find a way to make them look and feel woefully ill prepared. The class was pure torture.

Jack raised his hand. "I'm always open to new learning approaches. I think it's a great idea. I'll go first."

Louis responded, "All right, my man Jack will start us off. Just like in class, you present the book summary; take a position. Like Professor Wacmaster, I'll tell you why you're stupid. Let's start with Robert Quinn's book *Change the World*."

Jack began, "In his book *Change the World*, Richard Quinn explores business change management principles by looking at the lives of Jesus Christ, Mahatma Gandhi, and Dr. Martin Luther King, Jr. Quinn explains how these three men significantly changed the thinking of people. The book focuses on vision, unconditional confidence, and profound effect." He paused. "The book is sprinkled with examples of Jesus Christ, Mahatma Gandhi, and Dr. Martin Luther King, Jr. exhibiting these principles throughout their lives. Quinn makes the case that these three men were the most successful change agents in history. By following his eight principles, we mere mortals can be just as effective in initiating change of our own—"

Louis interrupted. "Yeah, yeah, so you've read the cover copy. Do you have a position, or do you intend to read the book to us?"

Jack resumed. "Well, I believe the book was well conceived and delivers actionable steps any aspiring leader can take to truly change the world. I believe the book is a good balance between leadership philosophy and pragmatism. There are so many worthwhile causes in the world; leaders would do well to follow the coaching and direction of Mr. Quinn."

Louis looked down his nose at Jack. "As soon as you raised your hand, I knew those words would come from your sophomoric excuse for a brain. You, sir, would have a better chance of graduating my class—which is quite improbable, I might add—than being able to execute any of the steps highlighted by Mr. Quinn. Furthermore, Mr. Quinn's ambitious effort misses the mark on many levels, the first of which is supposing mere *morons* like yourself could understand principles of—let alone emulate—Jesus Christ, Mahatma Gandhi, or Dr. Martin Luther King, Jr."

Louis paused dramatically before continuing his impersonation. "I'm sorry for being a bit presumptuous. Do you, sir, believe you can be like Gandhi? How about Nobel Peace Prize winner Dr. Martin Luther King, Jr.? You know we celebrate a national holiday because of Dr. King. Does Dr. King measure up to *your* greatness? Or are you planning to compare yourself with the savior of all humanity? Time itself is marked as before or after the earthly existence of Jesus Christ. Which one of these three men are you prepared to match résumés with after your casual read and elementary assessment of Mr. Quinn's book?"

Everyone froze. Louis had captured the essence of Dr. Wicco. It was as if he was possessed by the good doctor's soul.

Dorothy broke the silence to ask the question plaguing AU students for years. "Why does Wicco assign books he can always find a way to disagree with?"

Louis broke character to address Dorothy's question. "Because he's a demented, knuckle-headed professor with tenure." He was so confident in his response, he didn't pause for validation. With Jack in a daze, Louis gestured for the group to continue. "Which one of you *munchkins* wants to go next?"

Jack had finally recovered and was prepared to reassert his case. "Before we move on, Dr. Wicco, I must say although I'm not prepared to compare myself with the great men in Mr. Quinn's book, I believe it's possible and almost necessary to live by the eight change principles noted in *Change the World*. I believe what Mr. Quinn was telling us had to do with fundamental—"

Louis broke character again. "Jack, let me give you some advice—not as Dr. Weenie-head but as your friend, Louis. Give the guy what he wants, graduate, and move on with your life. The guy isn't worth the effort needed to change him. Your heart is big, Jack; for once use your brain."

Jack nodded to concede to Louis's logic. The group moved on to the next book of discussion.

Tim had been quiet for most of the evening. "I believe I've done a good job analyzing *Fierce Conversations* by Susan Scott. I'd like a shot at Professor Wicco."

"Ah, an intellectually stimulating analysis, I am sure," Louis said while emulating Wicco's familiar high-brow smirk.

Tim adjusted his Coke-bottle glasses and glanced at his notes as he began to summarize his reading of the book. With an engineer's precision and an executioner's machine gun–like rapid fire, Tim detailed his analysis.

"*Fierce Conversations* was written by Susan Scott in 2002. She focused on how to achieve success at work and in life one conversation at a time. *Fierce Conversations* has three transformational ideas. One, our work, our relationships, and our lives succeed or fail one conversation at a time. Two, the conversation is the relationship. Three, all conversations are with yourself, and sometimes they involve other people. Throughout the book the author focuses on seven principles and ten key ideas. Those are—"

Louis waved his hand to interrupt Tim while staying in character. "OK. OK, you've proven you read the book. Is there a *position* coming soon? Do you buy into the espousing of Ms. Scott?"

Tim looked at Jack. He looked at Louis again. Then he looked back at Jack.

Without making a sound, Jack mouthed the words "*don't do it.*"

"We are waiting," Louis said impatiently. "Are you willing to share your brilliance? Or do we need to read your mind? I am asking for your point of view on the book *Fierce Conversations*. What do you think? You do think, don't you?"

Knowing this was role-play didn't make it any easier to confront Dr. Wicco. Tim cleared his throat. "Of course I have a point of view. The question is, do you want *my* point of view or my interpretation of *your* point of view?"

The students uttered a collective low gasp. Even Tim was surprised the words had actually come from his lips. To think it was bad enough, but to say the words would change reality and create problems no previous Wicco student had dared to address.

Tim took a long look at Jack, who buried his head in his hands. He took a deep breath and summoned the strength to continue. "Well, professor, I believe this book is admirable but misguided. There is little room for leaders to wait and flex their communication to fit the preferences of those who are fortunate enough to have jobs in the first place. Ms. Scott talks about the *corporate nod* as if it were bad. Leaders deserve total commitment from the rank and file when it comes to executing. If frontline employees are so enterprising, they shouldn't be working for someone else. They can avail themselves of the free enterprise system and create their own business. Ms. Scott discusses *official truth* versus *ground truth*. As for me, the only truth is the one established by the person at the top of the org chart. No special insight into who the leader is *behind his or her mask* can change the fact that employees are there to execute as managers direct. Otherwise they can be replaced. Isn't unemployment up to eight percent?" Tim flashed a confident smile at Jack and Dorothy.

Louis recognized the cue to bring Dr. Wicco into the conversation. "Well, well, you have an opinion after all. *Avail themselves of the free enterprise system? Corporate nod? Official truth versus ground truth?* I must say, you have done an outstanding job of forming your point of view using the ideas introduced in the text."

Tim grinned and stood up to accept Dorothy's high five from across the table.

Louis cleared his throat as he continued his portrayal of Dr. Wicco. "As I see it, you have missed only two details. Both are so small, I hate to bring them up. For the sake of higher learning, please indulge me. First, unemployment is eight point two percent, not eight percent."

Tim, still smiling, nodded his acceptance.

Louis cleared his throat again, still focused on Tim. "Second, you missed the part about having your point of view make any sense whatsoever!"

Tim sat down with no sign of the smile that had previously occupied half of his face.

Louis continued as Wicco. "My good sir, when you are charged with leading organizations, you must remember you are leading fellow members of the human race. People have minds. People have thoughts. People have hearts—which is more than I can say for you. Are you supposing just because you are named CEO on a Monday, you will have all the answers on a Tuesday? What if you happen to be wrong about a portion of your strategy or a percentage of your calculation? Would you want someone to sound the alarm? Or should everyone follow you blindly over the cliff just because you are the boss? I know in your world, the numbers always add up. There is a problem if you are always the smartest person in the room. When you lead people, logic, order, and process only account for a portion of the calculus my friend—a small portion, I might add."

Dorothy and her friends were quiet for quite a long time. All one could hear was Miles Davis blowing in the background.

Louis smirked with confidence. "Come on, guys, you have to admit I nailed it. I worked in Wicco's *good sir* phrase and everything." To everyone's horror, Louis had captured perfectly the tone and tenor of a Dr. Wicco class.

Dorothy broke what seemed like an eternity of silence. "Well that's just great. Now I don't know what to expect. Louis just made a case for Wicco believing in servant leadership. Earlier I was convinced Wicco believed in command-and-control, autocratic leadership. I don't know what to think. We will never be ready for tomorrow."

Louis stepped out of character to remind Dorothy of his initial assessment of Dr. Wicco. "Dorothy, it's simple. Dr. Weasel-o only believes in torturing students. Like I said, he's a demented knucklehead with tenure."

Louis shook his head as he continued. "I see guys like him every year at the start of football season. They talk real tough during drills, lift a lot of weight in the workout room, and push the smaller players around for extra portions in the cafeteria. All is well and good until they have to click the chinstrap of a football helmet to back up words with action. Then it's a different story. Trust me, it's always a different story. You just can't show any fear. If you look them dead in the eye, *mano a mano*, they always back down."

Everyone remained in silence. Louis continued to beam in appreciation of his thespian-like performance and assessment of a Dr. Wicco. Ozzie came by to ask if they were ready for a refill. He said he wanted to make sure they were in good shape before leaving them in the capable hands of his night manager. "So, how goes the studying, guys?"

"Ozzie, it's not going well," Dorothy said with concern growing ever more evident on her face. "We know the material. Louis is doing a great job of pretending to be Professor Wicco. We just don't know what to expect on the exam."

Ozzie nodded and took a seat at the table.

Louis puffed out his chest, grinned, and waved, as if accepting applause from an audience of admiring fans. "Yeah, Mr. O., I have been bringing *da pain*. Unfortunately my friends here can't stand the heat."

Ozzie smiled as he looked over the books piled on the table. "These are some great books—*Jesus CEO* by Laurie Beth Jones, *Leading Change* by John P. Kotter, *The Art of War for Executives* by Donald G. Krause, *Outliers* by Malcom Gladwell. You could learn a lot about yourself if you actually did the exercises. Part of self-discovery is figuring out what you can be best in the world at doing. These books could guide your journey."

Ozzie picked up a DVD case sitting on top of the pile of books. "I love Marcus Buckingham. It's been a while since I've viewed these videos. As I recall, *Trombone Player Wanted* was the introduction to the strengths revolution. Buckingham believes strengths aren't just what you do well; they also reinvigorate you. They are activities you are actually strengthened by doing. Don't these videos explain how to apply those concepts in business and life?"

Dorothy reiterated the ongoing concern. "You're right about Marcus Buckingham. The problem is taking a point of view to earn an A on the exam. We're taking turns as Louis pretends to be Professor Wicco. No matter what we say, we can see Wicco saying we're wrong."

"I know Dr. Wicco a bit," Ozzie offered. "Who's next up to take a position?"

Since Louis was confident about being able to *beat Wicco at his own game,* they agreed they could benefit from watching him in action.

"What do you say, Louis?" Ozzie asked. "Are you game?"

Louis sprang to his feet. "Sure, I'm game. I've been waiting all semester to show you guys how it's done!" Louis looked at his friends, pointing a knowing finger at each of them.

Louis then looked down his nose at Ozzie. "Fair warning, though—don't think your being a cool coffee-shop owner will win any slack points for you. Once we step into the ring, you are no longer *Ozzie the wizard.* Even bringing Miles Davis back from the dead won't save you. To me you will be Professor Waste-o until someone yells, 'Cut!' or I hear you squeal like a cat with its tail caught in a bicycle chain."

Ozzie chuckled as if amused and agreed to Louis's terms. Dorothy, Jack, and Tim each grabbed a pen and directed their attention to Ozzie and Louis.

Ozzie lowered his glasses to the tip of his nose to begin his impersonation of Dr. Wicco. "Well, Louis, I understand you have studied Marcus Buckingham's work. Would you please enlighten your colleagues?"

Louis cleared his throat and flashed a half smile at each of his study partners. "Dr. Wac—um, I mean, Professor Wicco, I have given this a lot of thought. Considering the assigned reading and my outside research on the matter, I believe Marcus Buckingham's work is…well…whatever you think. Thank you!" Louis sat down quickly and picked up a magazine from the table.

After ten seconds of dead silence, Dorothy increased the silence by turning down the sounds of Miles Davis coming through the table speaker box. Without moving her head, her eyes slowly found their way back to Louis. "Excuse me…What in the *hell* was *that?*"

Louis sunk deeper in his seat, pretending spontaneous interest in a 1984 *National Geographic.*

Dorothy set aside her sweet Kansas innocence and sprang to her feet, pointing a finger at Louis. "You've talked all semester about what you would say to Wicco, *mano a mano,* and all you have is 'whatever you think'? You had Jack and Tim close to tears; all you give us is 'whatever you think.' Ozzie asks for your opinion, and you buckle and cower? I want to know what you have to say for yourself!"

Louis's imposing presence was reduced to a third of its usual stature. With all eyes on him, he lifted his eyes from the *National Geographic* ad on fly-fishing expeditions in the Amazon. In a voice more befitting a nine-year-old, Louis said, "Mr. O. was a bit too realistic. He scared me to death…and I need a good grade on this test to graduate. Who knows? If we show a little humility, we may soften the professor into feeling sorry for us. "

The quiet in the room was deafening. Even Miles Davis paused to begin a new selection.

Dorothy sat down, using a single finger to adjust her glasses. She murmured in a barely audible voice, "We are screwed."

Ozzie was next to speak. "In the late eighties, I saw a movie about a young stockbroker who lost his way chasing a rich client. One of the lines in the movie was something like, 'Man looks in the abyss; there's nothing staring back at him. At that moment man finds his character. That's what keeps him out of the abyss.' The line has meant a lot to me over the years. I sense you needed to hear those words tonight. I don't have a dog in this fight. After all I'm just a coffee-shop owner. I have seen this brand of panic many times in a previous life. In a few years, you'll look back on this and realize your highs weren't really that high, and your lows weren't really that low. The key is to use this experience to help you do what you believe is right. I have learned there are no shortcuts to success. Those who take the right actions for the right reasons are always rewarded."

Ozzie turned to Louis. "Before you decide to use *humility* as a strategy, you might benefit from hearing the best definition of humility I have heard. Many people believe to demonstrate humility, one must overacknowledge weaknesses and undervalue knowledge. Actually humility is acknowledging the reality of being human; that means unapologetically embracing your strengths as well as you own your flaws and shortcomings. Louis, no one is impressed by false humility, and no one is served by your hiding what you know or do well."

Ozzie wished them good luck on the exam. He told his night manager his friends' coffees were on the house. As he left, everyone continued looking at Louis, who had traded *National Geographic* for a 1993 issue of *Better Homes and Gardens*.

In a low, almost inaudible voice, Tim said, "Three hundred fifty thousand, three hundred twenty-one dollars and thirty-eight cents." He said it again slightly louder. "Three hundred fifty thousand, three hundred twenty-one dollars and thirty-eight cents. That's the cost of tuition and room and board at EWU. I did the calculation two years ago. I factored a two point five percent rate of inflation. Inflation has increased to three point seven percent and is compounded annually. Since a scholarship is soon to be out of the question, I'd better start looking for a job. I wonder if Ozzie could use some help here at Beans. With minimum wage at seven dollars and twenty-five cents, we're talking about only forty-eight thousand, three hundred twenty hours; maybe I can earn time and a half on holidays."

Louis tried to regain his normal persona. "Stop talking foolishness, guys. We know this stuff cold. We can do this. All we need to do is go into class tomorrow morning and show Dr. Weed-o who he's dealing with. I for one am going to—"

Dorothy leaped to her feet and lunged at Louis to cut him off mid-speech. "*You* are the *last* person I want to hear from at this moment. You are not even on the list of people I want to hear speak. Sit down, and say nothing until I give you permission to speak, Mr. Whatever-You-Think! *Comprende?*" It took Jack, Tim, and a large table to hold her back. Still, Louis took cover behind a nearby high-backed leather chair.

After Dorothy calmed, Jack reflected on the movie quote Ozzie had shared before leaving. "'Man looks in the abyss; there's nothing staring back at him. At that moment man finds his character. That's what keeps him out of the abyss.' What do you think Ozzie meant?"

With disgust, Dorothy opened another book piled on the table. She looked at Louis and adjusted her glasses. "He meant we're *screwed*."

THE EXAM

Morning had come far too soon. Students filed into the lecture hall to assume their usual seats. Dorothy and Jack sat two seats apart near the left side of Wicco's podium. Louis sat in the next to last row, in the third seat from the center. Tim was front row center. As the other students filed into the room, no one said a word. There was no buzz about last night's game. No one discussed the political issue of the day. No one commented on student fashion. Everyone looked as though they were about to see a ghost.

Wicco had a reputation for creating drama during finals time. Many thought he saw exams as his final opportunity to terrorize students. The room was completely still to the point one could hear the tick of the large black clock at the front of the hall.

Wicco was never late. Four minutes into the class, there was still no Wicco. One minute later Roxy Harris entered from the back of the room and walked to the front podium. With the room still, everyone heard the obviously rehearsed cadence of Roxy's boots as she marched to the front of the room.

Roxy was a second-year student and Wicco's teaching assistant. Wicco liked picking sophomores because they were mature enough to understand the significance of what he represented but had not taken enough core course work to understand everything discussed in class. Furthermore Wicco determined a former teaching assistant was useful for perpetuating the Wicco mystique among other students. A full year of horror stories among junior classmates contributed to the environment Wicco would artfully leverage their senior year.

Roxy wore a green coat with large black buttons and baggy green pants tucked into tall black boots. She topped off her look with white gloves. Lost on no one were the similarities to the Emerald City guards in *The Wizard of Oz*. When Roxy reached the front of the room, she had everyone's attention as she turned to face them. She pressed a button on a recorder no one had noticed sitting on Wicco's podium. Everyone heard Wicco's voice booming with perfect artistic diction, "Thank you, Roxy. You may leave now."

Roxy resumed her cadence as she left a classroom full of dazed faces. All eyes returned to the podium as Wicco's voice interrupted the silence. "Good morning, munchkins. I am sure everyone is well rested for today's assessment. You will need every minute of last night's rest to complete this assessment before the end of the hour. When finished, you will have until ten minutes after the hour to traverse to the northeastern corner of the room, where you will find an electronic lockbox. As you slide your assessment into the lockbox, your submission will be time stamped. Any assessment stamped outside of the ten-minute window will receive a fifteen-point deduction from its otherwise below-average grade. As you know, the top five percent will also receive my royal stamp of approval for a world awaiting their greatness. All others will begin their journeys into mediocrity. I will deal with cheaters using every means afforded to me by the rules and regulations of this university and to the extent I can avoid federal charges for torture."

After a dramatic pause, the recorded message continued. "As for this year's exam topic, I have decided to make it easy on you. Your essay will be on everything you have learned this year about leadership. In my calculation you now have fifty-two minutes remaining in class. The wise among you, assuming there are any, would want to begin writing *now!*"

The quiet was replaced by the sound of number-two pencils furiously leaving their marks. So much was riding on this exam for everyone in the class. Wicco made matters worse with his theatrics. The tension in the room was obvious. As the students completed their papers, they gave their work one last look before sliding it into the lockbox.

THE MORNING AFTER

Dorothy was awakened by the sound of someone sliding an envelope under her door. She gathered herself, grabbed a fluffy, sky-blue housecoat, and found her way to the door. Looking through the peephole, she caught a glimpse of Roxy Harris hurrying away. The envelope was bright yellow, with Dorothy's name handwritten on the front in blue ink. Dorothy looked up to see Roxy fading into the distance across campus.

"Boy, she's *moving*," Dorothy said aloud as she wiped the morning from her eyes.

Dorothy plopped back onto her bed and opened the envelope. Inside was beige stationery with the AU school crest in its upper left-hand corner. Written in the same blue ink were the words *"My office. Nine o'clock sharp. Wicco."*

Dorothy's face lost color as she thought, *Today is Saturday! Why does Wicco need to see me on a Saturday?* Speaking aloud to the dust bunnies who still occupied the corner, "Nine o'clock sharp? It's eight thirty now! How can I dress and cross campus in thirty minutes?" The dust bunnies shrugged, offering no solution.

Dorothy grabbed a pair of jeans and threw on her AU sweatshirt and a Kansas City Royals cap. She headed out with the yellow envelope, a snack bar, and a bottle of water in hand. Ordinarily she would walk the two hundred yards across campus to the administration building. Given Wicco's deadline, she would again call on Toto for help. Fortunately AU campus streets were desolate on Saturday until lunchtime.

As she drove she racked her brain for an inkling as to what Wicco might have in store. As she pulled up, she saw Tim and Jack talking to each other near the tall glass entrance of the administration building. Each clutched a yellow envelope with his name inked on the front.

Dorothy used her envelope to flag her friends' attention. She yelled their names as she left Toto in the parking lot. "Hey, guys! Do either of you know what this is about?"

Jack shook his head as he said, "I don't have a good feeling about this."

Dorothy asked, "Have you seen any other students go in with yellow envelopes?"

Tim said he hadn't seen anyone inside and that the door was still locked. The three friends pressed their faces against the glass window, trying to see through the smoky tint.

The lobby was decorated with old English wooden furniture, oil paintings of AU founder Austin Green, and a large, white-faced clock reporting it was 8:58 a.m. Just then they heard a blustering voice from behind.

"Wait for me-e-e-e! Don't go in without me!" Louis ran across the student quad complex at top speed with yellow envelop in hand.

Dorothy, Tim, and Jack were so focused on Louis, they didn't notice Roxy unlocking the door from inside the building. The clock ticked to nine o'clock as Roxy turned the last tumbler of the door lock. Dorothy, Tim, Jack, and Louis stepped inside.

Louis was out of breath. Sweating and panting like a wild animal, he made no attempt to camouflage his comments in whisper. "Do any of you guys know what the hell is going on?"

Tim gestured for Louis to lower his voice as each went in through the large glass doors. Tim turned to the group. "I am certain we're about to find out."

Roxy led the group down a long, dimly lit hallway. The hall ended with light creeping beneath an oversized wooden office door.

Jack reiterated his earlier concern. "I don't have a good feeling about this at all."

The group approached the large wooden door. Roxy stopped the group just short of it. She stepped forward and tapped the door knocker three times. Dorothy thought it was strange there would be a door knocker on an office door, but there it was.

"Sir, they're all here. Do you want me to bring them in, or should I have them wait?"

Louis leaned toward Tim. "How would you like to have her job?"

Wicco's voice bellowed from behind the door. "Enter!"

Roxy opened the door. The hinge squeaked loudly as the door opened. Almost simultaneously the four friends clasped hands. None of them had been in Dr. Wicco's office before. The room was full of autographed photos with inscriptions to Wicco. Some were of notable business executives; some were of athletes and movie stars. Dr. Wicco sat in a high-backed executive chair facing away from the door, gazing through a window overlooking the student quad.

Dorothy cleared her throat. "Sir, as Roxy said, we are here. None of us know *why* you—"

Wicco interrupted in a quiet but pointed voice. He lingered on each syllable with even more artistic flair than heard on the classroom recording. "Show manners to our guests, Roxy. Close the door behind you and wait in the lobby."

This time Tim leaned toward Louis. "I know I wouldn't want her job."

Hearing the squeak of the door close, Wicco spoke as he continued gazing out the window. "Would you like coffee or tea? I could have Roxy come back to pour a cup for each of you."

Dorothy swallowed hard and tried to pick up where she had left off. "No, sir. Thank you, though. I think I speak for my friends here by saying what we'd really like is to know why we're here. I mean, it *is* Saturday."

Wicco turned his head slightly to observe a different part of the student quad. "Ah, yes. So it is. Being it is Saturday, my good madam,

LEADERSHIP RESIDUE

and I'm sure each of you has important work to do, it would be rude of me to waste your time with civil pleasantries." Wicco remained facing the window but fixed his gaze on the reflection of his four visitors.

"I asked Roxy to bring you to my office so I could give you an opportunity to represent yourself. You, Dorothy—I figure you to be the leader of this cartel. Do you plan to represent the entire group, or will you serve as counsel only for yourself?"

The four exchanged puzzled looks before Dorothy stepped forward. "Represent? Counsel? For what, sir? I'm sorry, but I—I mean, we—still don't know what you're talking about...sir."

With a slow but pronounced whirl of his chair, Wicco turned around and tossed four packets of paper on his desk. "These! Would you care to represent yourselves as it pertains to *these*?"

Dorothy picked up one of the packets. "Well, sir, this one is the final exam I submitted for your class." Tim, Jack, and Louis validated the other three as theirs.

Dorothy handed the packet back to Wicco. "If that's all you wanted, sir, it seems like we could have just—"

Wicco turned his chair and his gaze back to the window. "It does not happen often. The theater I create is oft sufficient to keep everyone on the straight and narrow. Every few years one student is bold enough to take me on. Never have I had four in the same class." The friends looked at each other as Wicco continued. "It appears I have drastically underestimated this year's class. Indeed the whole lot of you appeared as ferocious as a bouquet of springtime pansies. Yet here we are. To say these assessments belong to each of you is a glaring proclamation of the obvious, my dear madam. What is not so obvious is how you did it." Wicco turned his chair to look at Dorothy directly.

Dorothy looked at the four stapled packets. "How did we do what... sir? I—I mean we—still don't know what you're talking about."

Wicco leaned back in his chair and allowed a smirk to spread across his face. "Seriously, Dorothy, you can save the country-bumpkin charm for your beloved Aunt Emily and Uncle Henry back in Blue Mound, Kansas, population two hundred fifteen. I am sure they have taken great care of Lucy, your prized cow, while you were here educating yourself in the big city."

Dorothy's confusion turned to amazement. "What are you talking about, and how do you know about Aunt Em, Big Hank, and Lucy?"

"I know all about your sad little story and the pitiful little admissions essay you wrote about raising your beloved Lucy. If it were not for one of the committee members swaying the others with a heartrending plea, you would not be here, my good madam. I was never fooled and voted against you from the start. Now I have the evidence I need. Soon enough you will be back in your rightful place, milking cows and peddling brown eggs at the farmers' market."

Dorothy put both hands to her heart and started to tear.

Louis came to her defense. "Hey, Wicco, you're going too far! Whatever game you have in mind, we're not playing!"

Wicco turned his attention to Louis. "Oh, really? I guess you would be our expert on the topic of *not playing*. With no prospect of an NFL career, I suppose you are just another crippled jock on campus looking for enough credit hours to graduate. I saw your SAT scores. Clearly AU did not realize its expected return on investment with you. Maybe now we can remove Coach Green from the admissions board once and for all. He is quite useless."

Jack perked up. "SAT scores aren't everything! SAT scores are biased to favor the privileged. I know many kids who have never seen a saucer, let alone know how its proximity to a table has anything to do with Saudi Arabia and Yemen. No one has to take the SAT to be successful."

Wicco shifted his glare to Jack. "How right you are. Of course, everyone has to *take* the SAT to be admitted to college. Right, Jack? I mean, do you care to produce your SAT scores? You don't, do you, because you never *took* the SAT. Some in this room might wonder how you were admitted to this fine institution without meeting the basic SAT requirement; everyone else did. Care to explain?"

With a puzzled look, Louis said quietly, "Yeah, I wouldn't mind hearing this myself."

Jack was boxed into a corner. He felt compelled to explain he couldn't take the SAT because he couldn't provide a home address on the registration form. He and his family had been homeless for eighteen months after his father was laid off. He was admitted as part of the state's temporary welfare-opportunity program. The program was disbanded due to the failure rate of many participants.

Tim was dumbfounded as well as embarrassed for Jack. "Aren't student files supposed to be sealed? You've just revealed student information to other students without permission. Wait until my grandfather hears about this. He'll make this a point of discussion at the next AU trustee meeting."

Jack, Louis, and Dorothy seemed to be of the same mind. In unison they cried, "Your grandfather!"

Wicco resumed his trademark sinister smile. "Yes, his grandfather is a trustee of this prestigious institution—one of the least influential trustees, I might add. Your grandfather cashed a big marker for you to come to AU—one might say his last big marker. It seems your friends are unaware of your poor track record with other universities. Is AU your third or fourth in three years? I bet your grandfather made it quite clear these were the last strings he would pull for you. How is your trust fund looking these days, Timothy? Are you sure you'll have access after your grandfather hears you and your friends have been expelled for cheating?"

"Cheating!" All four harmonized as if auditioning for Broadway.

THE ULTIMATUM

"You heard me. *In flagrante delicto.* All four of you have been caught in the act of committing a crime against this center of higher learning. I do not know how you did it. No one knew the essay topic except me until Roxy pressed *play* on the recorder. Somehow, all four of you provided strikingly similar essays, pulling from the same material discussed in class. You also referenced common themes *not* discussed in my class."

Dorothy looked at her friends' papers in more detail and read each title aloud.

Jack's title: "Scarecrow's Heart Reflects the Values of a True Leader." Tim's title: "The Tin Man and Other Great Leaders Use Their Brains to Acquire Knowledge." Louis's title: "It Is Impossible to Lead without the Courage of a Lion." Dorothy's title: "All I Know about Leadership, I Learned from *The Wizard of Oz*."

Dorothy dropped the papers, covered her mouth, and looked at her friends. She addressed Dr. Wicco again. "I admit this looks peculiar, but I assure you we didn't cheat. Sure, we studied together; many people study together. You said yourself we had no way of knowing the topic beforehand. We didn't even sit near each other during class. You can't expel us without proving we did something wrong."

Wicco paused and then looked at the ceiling. "You make a good point. Your assessments were ingenious efforts. Were it not for this question of integrity, each might be deserving of top scores. Although the probability of collusion is compelling, to prove cheating would be time consuming." Wicco paused as he turned his chair toward the window once again.

After another unbearably uncomfortable silence, Dorothy's reflection waved at Wicco in the window. "Professor Wicco? You were saying…" She leaned forward in a last attempt for the professor's attention.

Wicco turned the chair around with a smile slightly more pleasant than before. "Ah, yes, madam ringleader. Well, Dorothy, you have supported your case, and I am willing to make a deal with you. As you know, I have a highly regarded tradition of awarding A grades to the top five percent of all exams in the class." Wicco leaned back in his chair as if quite proud of the thoughts he was about to share. "I am willing to award an A to one of you, with all the accompanying benefits. The other three will receive their significantly below-average rightful grades. I will give you five minutes to confer among yourselves to determine who is most deserving. Roxy will come for you when your time has expired. I warn against testing my generosity."

Roxy touched Louis on the back of his arm. Louis jumped and shrieked. "How do you keep appearing out of nowhere?"

Without saying a word, Roxy motioned for all four to follow her back through the large wooden door. As when they had entered, the door squeaked as she pulled it open.

Louis looked back at his friends. "Seriously, where was that squeak a minute ago?"

THE ALTERNATIVE

Roxy returned to lead everyone back to his or her original positions across from Wicco's desk. Everyone held hands as they reentered the office. The door squeaked again.

Moving just his eyes, Wicco acknowledged Tim, Jack, and Louis. Then he returned his focus to Dorothy. "Well, Dorothy, let's begin this as we began the previous conversation. Will you represent the whole group or only yourself?"

Dorothy looked at each of her friends. "Sir, we have discussed it, and I am prepared to speak for all of us."

Wicco picked up the four essays and straightened them. He set them side by side on his desk. "Very well, then. To whom shall I bestow the coveted A grade?" Wicco picked up a red flare-tipped pen and posed as would a US president preparing to sign a bill into law.

Dorothy released the hands of her friends. "Well, Mr. Wicco—I mean Professor Wicco—with all due respect, we believe there is another option you might want to consider."

"Oh?" Wicco said as his raised his eyebrows ever so slightly.

The corners of Dorothy's mouth showed a hint of a smile. "Yes, I—I mean we—believe you will see this as an even better deal than the one you proposed earlier."

Wicco put down the pen and leaned forward ever so slightly. "Well, Dorothy, I must admit you have me intrigued."

Dorothy continued. "And for good reason, Professor Wicco, for good reason indeed." Dorothy assumed the midwestern spunk that allowed her to be so successful in student politics. Her smile dazzled. "We believe you should give us all As."

Jack, Tim, and Louis had been examining the patterns of the floor while Dorothy talked. Now they raised their eyes in search of Wicco's reaction.

Wicco picked up his pen again. "Quite amusing, Dorothy. Unfortunately, your offer is not on the table. I commend you for having well-written essays. I am willing to overlook the probable indiscretion. To whom shall I award my top score?"

Though seemingly impossible, Dorothy maintained her smile in the face of what most would consider bad news. "Dr. Wicco, I am so glad you see the situation as I do. Although I haven't seen my friends' papers, I know them as people. I'm not surprised to hear you say all of our papers are well written. Since they are all well written, we believe they all deserve As." She moved forward toward the edge of Wicco's desk. Her friends each took one step back.

Wicco chuckled. "You are quite the negotiator, Dorothy. I can see how others might be impressed by your poise at such a young age. Unfortunately, this is not a negotiation. But I admire your willingness to stand by your friends. Such virtue deserves a reward. Based on your performance here today, I will award an A grade to you and to the friend of your choosing. So who will it be, Dorothy? Who will join you in achieving the most valuable honor our university can bestow?"

"Thank you, Professor. I appreciate the kind words and the grade. You said yourself we all submitted work worthy of your compliments. Your reputation leads me to believe your compliments aren't easily earned. If our work is similar enough to cause you to think we cheated, our work should receive similar grades. We are all deserving of A grades."

The professor was no longer smiling. "I have seen this circus before. I warn you—your high-wire act has no net. You are asking me to compromise my grading policy. I am *not* going to award As, write endorsements, and place my personal stamp of approval on all of you. My decision is final." He looked at each of his students, this time with more than a passing glance.

Dorothy continued, "Sir, I am only asking you to do what's right. Assign the grades our work has earned. If you are concerned about the personal endorsement, I am willing to help. If you are willing to give each of us the grade we have earned…" Dorothy paused and looked at her friends. She looked at the photos of famous AU graduates sprinkled around Wicco's office. She saw businesspeople, senators, and judges—people she had long admired and people she didn't recognize. Dorothy realized the role Wicco could play in helping her achieve her long-term career goals—goals that a girl from Blue Mound, Kansas, could barely imagine.

She took a deep breath. "If you are willing to do what is right for my friends and me, I am willing to forgo the written endorsement for myself."

Wicco stared at Dorothy. "In all of my years, I have never received such an impassioned offer. Please explain to me why I should give this serious consideration. Why should I not follow my initial inclination to launch a cheating investigation against all of you?"

Dorothy walked to the side of the desk and looked through Wicco's window as she answered his question. "Well, that certainly would be an option. But in your heart, you know your approach wouldn't bode well for the reputation you have crafted among AU students, faculty, and alumni." Dorothy turned around so her back was to the window. All eyes were on her. With the poise of someone twice her age, she continued. "Dr. Wicco, you have taught us the importance of critical thinking. Because of you, we understand leadership is both skill and art. We learned as much from each other as we did from the books you assigned. We have learned that to be great leaders, we must have values in our decisions, build knowledge to remain relevant, and exhibit behavior to confidently reflect our values and knowledge."

Dorothy continued as if assuming the position of professor, with Wicco relegated to student. "You asked us to show all we have learned about leadership. From what I can tell, we have each met, if not exceeded, your expectation. We would make great ambassadors of your approach to developing leaders. How great would it be for us to say Dr. Wilson Wicco is demanding but fair? He is even willing to bend his own rules to build great leaders. What a wonderful lesson to pass along to future classes through an underclassman teaching assistant."

Everyone turned toward Roxy, standing by the door as a sentry might guard a royal court. She was so quiet, it was easy to forget she was listening to the entire conversation. Dorothy understood Roxy was Wicco's pawn. Now she attempted to use Wicco's pawn against him.

Wicco placed both elbows on his desk and clasped his hands is if preparing to arm-wrestle with himself. In a quiet but decisive voice, he broke the lingering silence. "Roxy, show our guests into the lobby for five minutes once more."

Roxy did as ordered.

PART 3
MOMENT OF TRUTH

Beans Wall Quote #162: "Authenticity is not something you have; it is something you choose."—Susan Scott

CLARITY

Dorothy emerged from her daydream as Tessie brought in coffee in preparation for a long evening.

"I thought you could use a fresh pot," said Tessie. "I don't know what it is about this coffee; it always clears my head when I need to think straight. Some say it's the fancy coffeepot. I don't think it makes sense to throw away three hundred dollars on a machine to basically boil water. For me, it's all about the beans." She placed the coffeepot on Dorothy's small wooden table.

Dorothy leaned back in her chair and gazed at her AU degree hanging on the wall. Then she murmured to herself, as if remembering a three-digit locker combination. "Man looks in the abyss; there's nothing staring back at him. At that moment, man finds his character. That's what keeps him out of the abyss. Your highs weren't really that high, and your lows weren't really that low. The key is to use the experience to help you do what you believe is right. There are no shortcuts; always try to take the right actions for the right reasons, and rewards will come."

Tessie was almost to the door when she turned to Dorothy. "Did you say something, hon?"

Dorothy smiled as she replied, "I think you're right, Tessie. It's all about the beans."

Tessie smiled as she left the office.

Dorothy looked at the picture she had taken with her friends outside of Beans. It had been years since they had talked seriously. Last she knew, through social media, they were all doing well. However, she missed having friends to talk with. The pursuit of the corner office had caused her to make choices—choices she couldn't have foreseen fifteen years ago.

It's funny, she thought. *It's hard to remember the homework assignments, special projects, and in-class exams.* It must have come easily. Certificates on the wall reminded her of graduating with honors. All she could remember was studying with those three friends.

Look how young everyone looks. Louis, Tim, and Jack. I miss those guys. The world seemed so simple then. It's hard to imagine we were stressed about anything—anything except Dr. Wilson Wicco. He made class a lot more complicated than it needed to be. All I can remember was the feeling of dread at the mere mention of Wicco's name. I'm losing my composure just thinking about his crazy antics. Although he seemed to have all of the answers, no one wanted to follow in his footsteps. I wonder if the dean ever fired him. If it wasn't for the coffee shop, we might never have graduated. I wonder if the shop still exists…

Now, Ozzie—he was the man everyone wanted to be. He created a wonderful environment for us to be ourselves and discover how we wanted to contribute to the world. We always felt smart just hanging out at Beans. He sure seemed to know who he was and what he stood for. Ozzie looked at everyone with a sense of hope and anticipation, like each one of us was destined for significance. I sure could use his thoughts on the BO Corp deal. I wonder what advice he would give. What would he think of how I've turned out?

Dorothy's face saddened a bit as she leaned back in her chair and sipped her coffee. *I have a lot more in common with Wicked Wicco than I do with Ozzie the Wiz. This is certainly not how I had mapped my journey to the corner office.*

With a spark of inspiration, Dorothy called Tessie back into her office. "Tess, I'm glad I caught you before you left. I need the team on the phone. I have an idea."

Dorothy looked through her window across to the bay. She continued to reflect on her career since AU. There had been a number of successes and failures. Each contributed to who she had become.

Dorothy thought about her first job in the technology industry. She had worked at E. Mill Corp as a customer service representative. Although college graduates may have felt entry-level sales were

LEADERSHIP RESIDUE 53

below them, Dorothy saw it as a break into the business. She took every training class and made friends in every department. She had an unquenchable thirst for knowledge and a passion for seeing everyone around her succeed.

Dorothy reflected on how much she enjoyed the family-oriented atmosphere at E. Mill Corp. There were company picnics and bowling tournaments. Everyone worked hard, played hard, and helped each other learn. In three years, Dorothy moved from telephone operator to associate VP of business development.

Success at a young age attracted weekly calls from employee-search firms. Soon, opportunities promised six-figure salaries and stock options. Not bad for a small-town farm girl from Kansas. Dorothy changed employers four times in the next nine years. With each career move came closer proximity to the corner office.

Three years was longer than she had anticipated staying with WB Tech. She was attracted by the SVP title and stock options. She stayed because she enjoyed the freedom Jeremy afforded her. Also, a part of Dorothy had come to believe holographic technology really could change the face of business. Her future could change within the next twenty-four hours—for better or for worse. A lot hinged on the technology and how well Dorothy could convince her audience of its possibilities.

Tessie peeked her head in the door. "I've found everyone. Hit line one when you're ready." She already had her coat on. Dorothy knew she would be alone for the rest of the night.

Dorothy took a deep breath before hitting line one. "Hey, guys. Before we start, I want to let you know how sorry I am for the drama I created earlier. I don't know how I've drifted so far from being the type of leader you deserve. I'd like to apologize and help you guys build a successful business case for Clone. Everyone has been working hard, and I suspect I've made this project a lot harder than it needed to be. If Clone materializes, it will be because of this group of dedicated engineers."

Dorothy paused before continuing. "I want to help. I'll stay as long as needed to help get us ready for tomorrow. Let me know what you need."

After a demanding moments of silence

After a demanding moment of silence, Matt cleared his throat. "Ah… um…well, quite kind of you to offer, Dorothy, but I believe we have everything under control."

"Really…everything under control?" Dorothy's tone suggested she wasn't a believer.

Matt continued without taking much of a breath. "Ah…yes! Nothing to worry about at all. Everything is under control. Well, almost everything. Just a few minor tests we want to run. You know, just as a precaution. We still have to test the connection quality when calling in late from every city. We also need to check the image quality during a reconnect. Sue brought up a good point about compatibility with the new three-D HDTV technology, so we want to test her assumptions as well." He continued talking until Dorothy cut in.

"Um, Matt, what you described doesn't sound like everything is under control. I know I've been acting like a real Wicked Bitch of the West. I want to help. I can't help if you won't level with me. I need to know *all* of the challenges we have with Clone. I want you to tell me everything." Dorothy's voice was calm but insistent.

Sue cleared her throat as she interjected. "No, we've made good progress. You shouldn't worry at all, Dorothy. We have twelve of our top engineers from around the world working through interface programming issues as we speak. They are prepared to work around the clock to make sure you have something to work with for your grand performance. There's a good chance—I mean, a one hundred percent chance—they will have the interface reprogrammed before your morning deadline."

"So you've found something wrong with the interface programming?" Dorothy's voice was still calm but increasing in pitch.

Larsen had been quiet during the call. Finally he butted in. "OK, OK, cut the crap, Dorothy! You made it clear we had until tomorrow morning to discover and fix all of the bugs with Clone. It's not eight in the morning yet. Give us time to work. I don't know what games you're playing here, but I for one don't buy your sudden conversion to softer, gentler leadership. We know how important tomorrow is to you and Jeremy. We know our jobs are on the line. You're eating up precious time with this charade."

Dorothy tried to edge a word in. "But I want to—"

Larsen didn't pause to hear Dorothy's plea. "We still have problems, OK? They aren't fixed! We know you have our replacements on speed dial. Unless you have anything new to threaten us with, we would all appreciate being able to spend whatever time we have left on this side of the unemployment line actually doing our jobs—you know the jobs you *overpay* us to do! As I recall someone saying earlier, the market isn't rich for washed-up engineers in their midfifties."

Dorothy tried again. "No, I really want to help. If you just give me a chance to hear what's going on, I might be able to—"

Larsen cut her off again, sounding desperate and frustrated. "Look, guys, you know where I stand, and you know how to find me. I've worked in this industry for twenty years and on this project for the last five years. I'm not ready to give up on something this important just because Jeremy and Dorothy can't get rich fast enough. Unless you hear Dorothy say I'm fired, call my cell if you come up with anything to move the project forward. I have real work to do in the lab. I've played on this call long enough."

Larsen's line clicked. It seemed like minutes before anyone else spoke.

Matt's manufactured laugh broke the silence. "Ha-ha, good old Larsen. The guy could make a killing on Comedy Central. He's just a little sleep deprived, that's all.

Matt continued. "Look, Dorothy, we're all in good shape. We just need to make a couple of minor tweaks, but everything will be in good shape by eight o'clock tomorrow morning. You go home, and have a good night's rest. After all, tomorrow is your big day. You want to be at your best."

Dorothy hated when her words came back to bite her. She knew she was too far down the path now to be part of the solution. She left the group to their hard work.

MEETING WITH JEREMY

Dorothy began the morning by perusing her e-mails. As expected there were dozens of e-mails from her team indicating that Clone was up and running. The team knew to comply with Dorothy's demands. She didn't know how much of the e-mails' optimism to believe.

Dorothy spoke aloud as if providing coaching to the computer screen. "The problem with compliance is, at best, you get only what you ask for."

Dorothy was copied on several e-mails regarding Clone. Her team did whatever they could to protect themselves against blame. E-mails were time stamped at various times throughout the night and early morning. Most of the activity was prior to 5:00 a.m.

One e-mail from BO Corp confirmed the list of attendees for the eleven o'clock meeting. The list looked like a full roster of the BO Corp executive team. Even their CEO was returning early from a family vacation to attend. He would arrive toward the end of the meeting with enough time to shake hands before being whisked off to another engagement.

Jeremy e-mailed Dorothy an update on his travel. He wanted to meet at a Starbucks a few blocks from the BO Corp office. He suggested ten o'clock to review the role he needed to play in the meeting.

Jeremy religiously avoided the unpredictable flow of customer meetings. He liked the security of the WB Tech innovation lab. Given this was such a big opportunity, though, Dorothy made it clear his presence was critical.

Jeremy had worked on this technology for close to a decade. For the last three months, however, he had diverted his focus to new innovations. Eduscope was technology to allow teachers to monitor student brain activity in real time. Outside of agreeing to attend this meeting, Jeremy had all but turned over Clone to Dorothy.

Dorothy felt bad about how the session with her team ended. She was sure they only told her what she wanted to hear. Now she had to trust her team's work and that Clone would actually deliver what she was about to sell to BO Corp.

Dorothy walked into the Starbucks at nine thirty. The aroma brought her back to simpler times—times when friends were plentiful, great music was free, and the coffee was incredible. This was the second time in twenty-four hours she had reflected on Beans and her college friends. Instead of sipping dark roast from a small Colombian grower, today she enjoyed a full-bodied Caffé Verona. Instead of Miles Davis's muted horn over the loudspeaker, it was Jamie Cullum's jazzy version of "Don't Stop the Music." It dawned on Dorothy how much had changed over the last fifteen years. Chief of all changes was her life. In college she had been concerned about passing a class. Today she would make the deal of her career. Despite all of her success, she still longed for family and friends.

Just as she was nearing the bottom of her cup, Jeremy arrived. As usual he was punctual. Dorothy noticed he was dressed a lot more formally than typical. Clearly he had thought through every detail of what to wear, down to the gold cuff links. Even with all of the Brooks Brothers polishing, Dorothy could tell he was uncomfortable.

"Boy, you clean up well." Dorothy met Jeremy halfway across the floor.

Jeremy ran his fingers through his hair and allowed his hand to linger on the back of his neck. "You know me. Give me a computer screen and a few engineers, and I am ready to go. This schmoozing stuff is why I pay you."

MEETING WITH JEREMY

Dorothy flashed a knowing smile, hoping to calm Jeremy a bit. She pulled out a chair and gestured for him to take a seat. "I know, I know. If it weren't business critical, I wouldn't ask you to come. One of my industry contacts said BO Corp likes to know the people behind the businesses they deal with. They asked about meeting you three times already. This is the first time I've insisted you join."

Jeremy took a seat, careful not to wrinkle his suit. He talked quickly when excited; this was no exception. "I'm just glad this is the last time I have to do this for Clone. With this deal we can monetize the project and focus all of our attention on building the infrastructure around Eduscope. You know, we're making real breakthroughs. Pretty soon I'll bring you in on the technology side so you can start thinking about the business case. We've just finalized the corporate documents for Eduscope LLC. This separates our new technology from Clone—and WB Tech. The biggest challenge for us will be working with the education bureaucracy to make this a national mandate. You would think with all of the negative press about the challenges of educating youth, this would be easy. No, this is going to be a fight. I'm only glad I'll have you leading the way. Do you have contacts in government to leverage the school boards?"

Dorothy leaned forward, as if sharing a secret with an old friend. "I have a great idea."

Jeremy looked around and leaned in to match Dorothy's posture. His eyes took on a schoolboy sparkle. "Already thinking ahead, huh? What thoughts do you have? Who do you know? What first steps should we take for Eduscope?"

Dorothy leaned in even more and cupped her hand around her mouth to further conceal her secret. She whispered, "Clone."

Jeremy's expression changed to intrigue. "Clone? How can Clone help us with Eduscope? The technologies aren't complementary at all."

Dorothy leaned back and spoke in her normal tone. "We're here to make Clone a success. Before we start talking about the *next* big thing, can we focus on *this* big thing?"

Jeremy sat back as his boyish grin dissipated. "I suppose you're right. I may be a little ahead of myself. My monkey suit and I are here to support Clone. What do I need to know? What will you need me to do?" He looked sheepishly at Dorothy.

Dorothy paused and looked directly into Jeremy's eyes. "First, thank you for wearing the monkey suit. BO Corp is a bit formal. Second, all I need you to do is look presidential. Talk about why you were compelled to create the technology. What guiding principles underpin the development? Basically just recite the stuff we put on our website. I'll handle the rest."

He looked relieved. "I can tell my story with no problem. As for looking presidential, all I have is this twelve-hundred-dollar monkey suit. For twelve hundred dollars, this suit should *be presidential*."

Dorothy smiled. "As for what you should know, we had a few glitches with the interface in last night's dry run. The team assured me we're ready to go for the live demo."

Jeremy picked lint from his suit sleeve and tugged at the collar of his shirt. "Let's hope so. I would hate to have dressed up and traveled all this way for nothing. Once we can fully fund Eduscope, we can staff up with real engineers. Aren't most of those guys on your team in their fifties? I bet their idea of fun is programming BASIC on Commodore Sixty-Four computers."

Dorothy was shocked to hear Jeremy talk so poorly about the team who had worked so hard to bring his dream to life.

Jeremy must have noticed Dorothy's blank stare and tried to redeem himself. "Come on, Dorothy. I'm not saying anything you haven't thought yourself. I admit they were the best I could afford on a shoestring budget. We close this deal with BO Corp, and we can afford real talent. You know, smarter, more relevant engineers who can prepare us for the future. Today's talent can do more with a tablet and a smartphone than your current team can even dream of. If they think the interface for Clone is complex, they wouldn't last two weeks on Eduscope."

Jeremy paused. "Don't worry about your team. With the money we make on today's deal, we'll float each of them a nice bonus. I have three second-level venture capitalists lined up, just waiting to hear the results of today's meeting. They'll buy WB Tech, recapitalize, and staff the entire operation. We just have to demonstrate Clone has the ability to be a billion-dollar technology."

Dorothy looked at her watch and stood up. She wanted to end the conversation and indicate it was time to leave. Jeremy followed. She hadn't anticipated growing attached to her team. Even with all of her demands, she knew how devoted they were. They weren't dedicated only to Clone but also to the company. It was hard for Dorothy to hear her team would be easily discarded. It might only be a matter of time before she would be discarded as well. She realized her hard work would mean nothing if Jeremy decided it was time for changes without her.

PROPOSAL AT BO CORP

For nearly forty-five minutes, Dorothy eloquently made the case for holographic technology being the intercom of the future. BO Corp executives were captivated by her energy and command of the room. She ended the first portion of the presentation with the famed tagline, "Why would you risk your global expansion to the inconsistencies of video when you could send a Clone?"

The room warmed with smiles. Everyone nodded in agreement. Taking his cue, Jeremy took the floor. "We have brought holographic technology beyond what was described in the sci-fi comic books of my youth. I wanted to make it real. I believe there was a moment when da Vinci and Newton each realized they had put flesh on their imagination. Ladies and gentlemen, I join them in this moment. I am excited to share this moment with BO Corp. We are at a moment future generations will read about in their history books."

Although he was clearly outside of his comfort zone, Dorothy thought Jeremy's performance was brilliant. It was just what she had hoped.

Dorothy resumed the spotlight. "I think we've done enough talking. How would you like to see the technology in action?" She flipped a switch, turning on the televisions positioned around the room. All at once four faces appeared from four corners of the world. The faces belonged to BO Corp executives in London, Santiago, Monterey, and Shanghai. Looks of astonishment were on all four faces. At one point all reached for the screens as if attempting to touch Dorothy's holographic image once she stepped into view of the transmitters. The room erupted in laughter and applause.

The BO Corp CEO arrived as the demonstration was in progress. Dorothy invited him to replace her in the view of the transmitters. His holograph was then in four offices at once. He clapped his hands and pumped his fist as would a playground soccer player scoring his first goal. The CEO addressed his virtual audience.

"Like Neil Armstrong, today we stake our flag in the next frontier."

The room exploded with even more applause.

The CEO gave a nod to Jeremy and turned to Dorothy. "This is just the technology we are looking for to cement our competitive edge in the marketplace and improve employee engagement. I commend you and your team for pulling together such an impressive demonstration. We have looked at the preliminary numbers, and we appear to be in the ballpark. If you can support our expansion plans, you can count on us as a partner. How soon can you install a Clone in every BO Corp office?"

Jeremy stood up as if to close the deal. "We can definitely support your expansion needs. We have the best and the brightest engineers ready to make sure you succeed. You give us the go-ahead, and we can put this in place in every BO Corp office around the world thirty days after we formalize our agreement." Jeremy's excitement matched the BO Corp CEO's.

Dorothy cleared her throat to gain the CEO's attention. "We are certainly glad you see a fit for Clone in your plan for the future. Before you commit to spending millions of dollars to put a Clone in every office, I wonder if you might be open to evaluating an alternative."

The CEO turned his attention to Dorothy, curious about her comment. Dorothy knew this was a big opportunity. She felt a need to slow down the process a bit. She hadn't personally tested the interface issues found less than twenty-four hours ago. She had pushed her team pretty hard; would they tell her if other issues were discovered? If the fix wasn't fully vetted, there could be extensive service and retrofitting expenses later on. In addition there could be an enormous amount of negative press for Clone and WB Tech on the back end if implementation was less than flawless.

Jeremy's glowing smile dissipated. "Alternative? There's no need to discuss alternatives if Clone meets the needs and you're ready to formalize the deal. My attorneys can have the contract available for your signature by the end of the week."

One of the BO Corp executives asked, "Alternatives? I think I would like to hear what Dorothy has in mind."

Jeremy shot Dorothy a look of disbelief. She cleared her throat again and resumed the spotlight. "Clone is a fantastic technology. I certainly believe everything I said earlier, especially the part about helping you create a sustainable competitive advantage in the market. While we can make this happen for you and deliver Clone to all of your current offices, I wonder if there could be...well, more."

Another BO Corp executive sought to continue the exploration. "More? More like what?"

Dorothy walked to a framed poster of an old America map. She paused before continuing. "What made Christopher Columbus so amazing was that he didn't ascribe to everyone's beliefs about the world in his time. He was willing to travel the world in search of more. He didn't know what more was; he merely believed it was out there. Fortunately for all of us in this room, he was able to inspire Queen Elizabeth to fund his search for more. Columbus and Queen Elizabeth did not settle. I propose you not settle. I propose you join us in our search for more."

Dorothy walked toward the BO Corp CEO. "You said today you stake the company's flag in the next frontier. Don't you want more than just a flag on a hill? What if you could own the entire frontier?"

The BO Corp CEO sat down in a nearby conference-room chair and leaned back just a bit, as if contemplating the story Dorothy was building.

Dorothy continued. "Shortly after writing the check to WB Tech, I am sure you will issue a press release announcing our partnership. We will thank you and fill your order. We will do everything in our power to make Clone a success for your organization. Do you know why? Because our success as a company depends on our ability to collect a strong review from you—a review we can use to acquire new customers and new investors."

By this time Dorothy seemed to be holding a one-on-one conversation with the BO Corp CEO. Looking intrigued, he responded, "If everything works as well as demonstrated today, and the financials are as my CFO suggests, we would be happy to give you a recommendation. We will even work with your advertising team to develop a fully integrated campaign if you would like." His smile still showed hints of being confused.

Dorothy crossed her arms as she stepped toward a window overlooking a grassy lawn. "So if you were a competitor of BO Corp, how long would you lose market share and talented employees before you sought out a holographic technology of your own? One year? Six months? Less?"

Dorothy turned to one of the well-dressed executives in the room. "You, sir, you with the pretty yellow tie. You are young and obviously have a good head on your shoulders to have made it so far in an organization as dynamic as BO Corp. Do executive recruiters ever call you with opportunities?"

The executive wasn't prepared for the politically charged question. "Of course they call; they call all of us. I don't answer those calls, though. I just let them go to voice mail, or I pass them along to my friends." The executive looked around the room, ending with a tentative glance toward his CEO.

Dorothy walked toward the young executive. "What if the next call comes with an offer of ten thousand dollars more than your current salary? What if it offers twenty thousand dollars more and a corner office? Would you answer the call? Would you be willing to at least have the conversation to see where it might lead?"

Dorothy put her hand on the young executive's shoulder to indicate he was out of the hot seat. She then turned back to the CEO. "I join you in believing holographic technology will change how the world communicates. It will do what cell towers and satellites have done for telephone communication. It will do what combustible engines did for ground transportation. It will do what microbiology did for medicine. No other firm has made the progress we've made in this field. There are other firms out there; they just haven't thought to do what we've done. But a holographic conferencing technology alone will not drive employee engagement."

Jeremy's face was a mix of shock and frustration. "If you have a point, I am sure everyone here would appreciate hearing it. We are dangerously close to our time limit." He tugged at his collar as beads of perspiration began to form on his brow.

Dorothy kept her eyes fixed on the BO Corp CEO. "My point is this. None of us knows the future. We don't know what opportunities or challenges might come our way. All any of us can do is make the best decisions today to stay ahead of competitors who might come after us tomorrow. Engaged employees stay with companies who encourage them to make meaningful contributions. You keep Mr. Pretty Yellow Tie here from answering the recruiter's call by showing him BO Corp is prepared to make bold moves to support his future. Do this, and the money will not matter to the high-potential employees you really want to keep. Investing in snappy technology in the name of employee engagement is playing it safe. Sir, don't play it safe."

The CEO stood up and folded his arms in a way reminiscent of a John F. Kennedy portrait. "Well, if investing millions in cutting-edge technology is playing it safe, what would you call bold?"

Dorothy surveyed the room. All heads were leaned forward, with all eyes on her. She had successfully captured everyone's attention. Everyone listened, including Jeremy, who was noticeably gritting his teeth beneath pursed lips.

"Don't just buy our technology, sir. My alternative is for you to buy our technology and our company."

Quiet suffocated the room like a ton of feathers in a telephone booth.

THE RESPONSE

Dorothy couldn't believe the words she had just said. She wasn't quite sure from where the idea had come. She realized she was out on a limb and couldn't climb back to the safety she had known. So she continued her explanation.

"By purchasing WB Tech, you own Clone, you employ the engineers who commercialized the technology, and you benefit from all of the improvements made on the current system. Instead of announcing you've purchased technology, you announce you've purchased a technology firm. While your competitors are stalking technology companies in Silicon Valley in search of a way to compete, you'll have an in-house team of seasoned engineers working on the next innovation to sustain your competitive advantage."

The BO Corp CEO raised one of his arms to tap a finger to his chin. He looked at Jeremy, who tugged at his collar again. The CEO looked back at Dorothy.

"It is an intriguing alternative. Unfortunately we don't have the appetite for technology acquisitions right now. I was under the impression this meeting was about helping us with communication and improving employee engagement as we expand globally. If this is merely an acquisition proposal, I am afraid we will have to schedule time with our mergers and acquisitions team on a different day."

Dorothy's cool demeanor cracked. "Look, sir, I know this isn't what you had planned. This isn't exactly what we had planned. We have extremely talented engineers, and this is a real opportunity for you to—"

Jeremy stood up and addressed the BO Corp CEO directly. "Please excuse the creativity of my marketing executive. As you've seen, Dorothy is bright and has a lively imagination. This is the first time I've known her exuberance to cloud her business judgment. Let's not let this episode stand in the way of our partnership. You tell us when and where you would like the first shipment of Clones, and Dorothy and I will make it happen."

Dorothy's energy increased as she moved closer to the CEO. "Don't be shortsighted, sir. This can be so much more than—"

Jeremy cut Dorothy off again. "Enough, Dorothy! In fact I can handle the discussion from here…if you wouldn't mind waiting for me in the lobby."

As Dorothy left the conference room, she could hear Jeremy apologizing to the BO executive team again. He even guaranteed no further mention of a WB Tech acquisition. Dorothy knew this was the end of her career at WB Tech. She paused in the lobby only long enough to leave the rental car keys with the receptionist. She asked her to give them to her colleague when he emerged from the conference room.

PART 4
NEW BEGINNINGS

Beans Wall Quote #117: "I've learned that people will forget what you said, people will forget what you did, but people will never forget how you made them feel."—Dr. Maya Angelou

MONTHS LATER

Dorothy came back to her condo after a morning run. She had come to enjoy the time to herself. She never considered herself to be a runner—or an athlete at all.

It had been months since her meeting at BO Corp. She still hadn't opened the boxes from her office or deleted the messages on her answering machine. Many of the messages were from former team members. It didn't take long for stories to circulate about how she'd nearly jeopardized the deal responsible for turning Clone into a billion-dollar brand. Although they were out of a job, they thanked her for trying to ensure a home for them as part of BO Corp.

A press release and advertising campaign lauded the magical connection between BO Corp and WB Tech. With this recent success, Jeremy attracted more attention from *Fast Company, The Wall Street Journal,* and *Businessweek.* There was no mention of Dorothy. Jeremy had no problem attracting investors. He recapitalized the firm. All of the engineers were replaced by smart, young graduates from the top technology schools.

Dorothy sipped her coffee and glanced over the newspaper. Months ago, if she had taken the time to read the paper, she would have turned straight to the business section. Now she spent entire mornings reading everything from lifestyle to community happenings. She hadn't begun looking through the want ads. Every time she thought about her next career move, she would sink into self-doubt and despair. Her time at WB Tech hadn't ended how she had imagined. Not only did she not move any closer to the corner office, but she was also left to wonder how she would live beyond the final bonus and options.

In the fast-paced world of corporate technology, Dorothy never took time to consider what she wanted beyond a corner office and a paycheck. If only she had someone who could tell her what to do next.

As she took another sip of coffee, she noticed her framed AU diploma sticking out of large white partially opened box. She reflected on how sure her future had been in college. She would give anything for even a fraction of confidence today. As she sipped at her coffee, she remembered something Ozzie had said the night before their Wicco exam: "*These are some great books. You could learn about yourself if you actually did the exercises. Part of self-discovery is figuring out what you can the best in the world at doing.*"

Unemployment afforded only one real benefit: time to reflect. Dorothy searched for her college books. She found more than enough to start a journey of self-discovery. This time she would do the work not for a grade but for herself.

Just like in college, she piled all of the books on her kitchen table, brewed another pot of coffee, and summoned Miles Davis on her computer. Minutes turned into hours, and hours turned into half a day. Before she knew it, the sun was going down as she raced through the books. She read, highlighted, and underlined and added notes to a journal. The sunrise reminded her that she hadn't eaten for the entire day.

This was to be her articulation of who she wanted to become as a leader. She detailed lifelong beliefs and core values. She could've easily replaced Tom Cruise in the opening scenes of the movie *Jerry Maguire*. She too was developing a personal manifesto.

Books from Susan Scott, Simon Sinek, Marcus Buckingham, and the like helped her cause. Dorothy did every exercise and completed every chart. She reviewed feedback of how others experienced her leadership. She defined for herself what it meant to be authentic and in integrity with herself. It was more than a mission statement. It was a leadership platform, a bold declaration of how she planned to positively influence anyone willing to follow.

A phone message broke her laser-like focus on her document of self-discovery. A vaguely familiar voice complemented the muted trumpet of Miles Davis, still playing in the background.

"Hello, Dorothy. This is Bill. I was one of the BO Corp executives you met with a few months ago. You know, the one wearing the pretty yellow tie? I hope you don't mind my calling. I searched all over the city and the Internet for your number. Anyway, I would appreciate it if you would give me a call when you can. I want to talk to you about a project I am working on. It has a time limit, so I need to talk to you soon."

The message ended, and Dorothy was momentarily unable to move. She thought it was odd for a BO Corp executive to want to speak to her. She wrote down his number, attached it to the refrigerator door with a magnet, and returned to her computer. She spent another twenty hours refining and massaging her document to help test Ozzie's assertion of "the universe conspiring to help people achieve clearly articulated goals."

Without looking, she reached for the coffeepot for a quick burst of inspiration. It was empty again. She proofread a printed version of her work as she walked to the cabinet where she kept emergency packages of her specially ground coffee beans. To her surprise she had exhausted her entire supply.

"Well, this just won't do," she said. "Looks like Thoreau will have to leave Walden after all."

Dorothy grabbed her car keys and phone and tucked her curls under a Kansas City Royals cap. It was a short trip to a local coffee shop.

THE GRIND

Dorothy loved coming to this coffee shop. It was locally owned and reminded her of simpler times. The coffee was good, the baristas were friendly, and the consumers beamed with optimism. There were lots of great books to read. When she could, she spent entire mornings there. This morning was different, especially for a Saturday. She was on a mission. She wanted to return to the task of discovering what she wanted in her life and career. The short drive inspired additional thoughts for her platform. Also different was that she hadn't showered in three days.

She picked up the two whole-bean elements of her favorite blend and handed them to the barista. As she waited, she tried to type her current thoughts on her smartphone.

A man's voice pierced her concentration. "Dorothy, is that you?"

Dorothy was petrified to think of being recognized on the one day she wasn't prepared to be social. She tugged at the bill of her cap and tried to continue typing. Her only hope was there might be another Dorothy in the coffee shop.

"Dorothy, it is you, isn't it?"

She tried to disappear under her cap and into her smartphone.

As the man walked closer, Dorothy's fears were validated. She was the Dorothy he was calling. Unfortunately for Dorothy, the man continued to come closer.

"It's me, Bill. I just left you a voice mail. What are you doing in this part of the Bay?" It was Bill from BO Corp. Dorothy hardly recognized him, partly because his gray hoodie was far less formal than what he'd

LEADERSHIP RESIDUE

won the last time they had met and partly because she was trying to avoid direct eye contact, given her current condition.

Realizing there was no way to avoid the conversation, Dorothy fully extended her arm to shake his hand. "Oh my, Mr. Pretty Yellow Tie. Yes, it's me. I have a condo not far from here. You?" Dorothy was trying to be polite without getting close.

"I'm not far either. I love coming to this place on Saturday mornings. It helps me clear my head. Don't you just love the vibe?" Bill unzipped his hoodie, ran his fingers through his hair, and flashed a brilliant smile as he looked around.

"Yeah, and the coffee's not bad either." Dorothy looked toward the barista, psychically willing him to call her name and end this professional nightmare.

"Yeah, the coffee's not bad. It's not as good as I had back in college. I didn't know how good I had it. There must have been something about those beans after all." Bill turned toward the menu to contemplate his order.

Dorothy perked up and took a longer look at Bill. "Excuse me, what did you say?"

Bill ran his fingers through his hair again, not shifting his focus from the menu. "There must have been something about those beans. It's just and old tag line for a coffee shop just off campus at my alma mater."

Dorothy glanced at the college T-shirt peeking out behind the open zipper of Bill's hoodie. "Don't tell me you're an AU Flying Monkey reminiscing about Beans."

Bill seemed surprised. "I am. I graduated six years ago. Not many people have heard of AU around here."

"I am an AU alumna myself. I've been out much longer than six years, though." Dorothy showed a glimmer of the smile she used to captivate Bill and the other BO Corp executives only months ago.

Dorothy and Bill exchanged a few memories about their AU experiences. Bill had just returned from his class reunion and was able to update Dorothy on campus changes, new professors, and football recruits for the upcoming season.

"Hey, what ever happened to Beans? I've been thinking about looking up Ozzie. Is he still around?"

The barista called Dorothy's name to indicate her order was ready.

"You won't believe it; they replaced Beans with a Starbucks three years ago. It was never the same after Ozzie died."

"Ozzie is dead?" Dorothy clutched her chest in disbelief.

Bill tried to comfort Dorothy. "He must have been seventy-five or eighty years old. My cousin was an AU senior when it happened. She told me about the crowd of people who came by the chapel to pay last respects. Supposedly even Dr. Wicco cried while delivering the eulogy."

Dorothy grabbed her coffee order, still unprepared for the conversation she was having. "Wicco delivered his eulogy?"

"Yeah. It turns out he and Ozzie roomed together in grad school at EWU. They attended each other's weddings and golfed together in the summers." Bill turned to the barista to place his order.

Dorothy gazed across the room. "I was just thinking about advice Ozzie gave me my senior year."

Bill echoed her sentiments. "I think about him myself from time to time, especially when I'm torn over tough choices. Ozzie was full of timeless advice. He always seemed confident—a real gift for him, I guess. Guess he was trying to make up for past sins."

Dorothy leaned in to hear the scoop of the century. "Make up for past sins?"

Bill elaborated. "Well, Ozzie didn't always have his trademark wisdom and great judgment. Before Beans he was a senior executive at an East Coast consulting firm. The CEO made off with millions of dollars earmarked for employee profit sharing. Ozzie received a payday as part of the scam. To receive a suspended sentence, he repaid the money and ratted out the CEO. That basically ended his corporate career. Since he partnered with the government, they cleared his history and kept it out of the papers."

Dorothy tugged at the bill of her hat and adjusted her glasses before leaning in to continue the conversation. "If they kept this all top secret, how did you find out?"

LEADERSHIP RESIDUE 77

Bill flashed a devilish grin. "I married one of Wicco's TAs. She told me everything. Come to find out Wicco was one of the few people Ozzie confided in."

Still dazed by all the news, Dorothy thanked Bill for the AU update and headed toward the door.

Before he got there, Bill called for her to wait. He paid for his double latte and trotted to meet her halfway.

"I almost forgot. I called you because I'm working on a project you might be able to help with."

Dorothy reminded him she no longer had anything to do with Clone or WB Tech. Bill explained he was working on a project for his uncle's executive recruiting firm. He said he thought she might be a good fit given her background and knowledge and the passion she had exhibited at BO Corp headquarters.

"I could be interested. What's the company, and what's the role?" Dorothy dropped her beans when Bill told her it was E. Mill Corp. They were looking for someone to head up a new division in emerging innovations.

LESSONS FROM THE JOURNEY

Dorothy loved being back at E. Mill Corp. Even more, she loved her role. She didn't mind her salary being less than what she had made at WB Tech. In the nine months she had been back, she had built an organizational structure and almost completely staffed her team. Many of her old colleagues were still there but in more senior positions. She and her team of nine senior business development managers scoured the globe for cutting-edge innovation poised to generate $1 billion in annual net revenue. She quickly regained her reputation for being a highly engaged leader with a keen focus on developing and inspiring others. It was as if she had never left. Only she *had* left.

In the time she had been away, she had learned the dangers of chasing a title and a paycheck. She had also learned the importance of investing in others. More important she had learned the value of being authentic and transparent. One could hear employees reciting a "Dorothy-ism" from any corner of the organization. She felt like it *mattered* she was there and not somewhere else.

A particularly exciting day for Dorothy was the day she met with Tessie—the same Tessie who had worked with her at WB Tech. After Jeremy closed the WB Tech office, Tessie decided to go to school full time. She was nearing the end of the LCC associate's program. She connected with Dorothy on social media. They met monthly to discuss her classes, business, and life in general. Dorothy enjoyed teaching what she knew as much as Tessie appreciated the mentoring.

LEADERSHIP RESIDUE

Dorothy's eyes sparkled when Tessie came into the office. "Tess, today I want to discuss the topic of leadership."

Tessie smiled. "Great. I've always wanted to know how to make people do what I want them to do. You know, like you did back at WB Tech."

Dorothy's eyes lost their sparkle. "Tess, if there's one thing I've learned, it's that leaders can't *make* people do anything. What I did at WB Tech was closer to assault than leadership. Effective leadership inspires people to want to follow. Truly inspiring leaders leave a positive residue."

With a puzzled look on her face, Tessie repeated, "Residue? I've only heard of residue being something you work hard to remove, like the film left over after a glass of milk. I've never heard of leadership residue."

Dorothy pulled out a yellow legal pad as she began to answer Tessie's question. "Leadership residue is just as it sounds. It's the influence a leader leaves to impact behavior after he or she has gone. Let's begin by discussing the three primary responsibilities of leaders." Dorothy drew three bullet points and wrote two words after each bullet point: "Picture Success," "Inspire Action," and "Remove Barriers."

> **Picture Success**
> **Inspire Action**
> **Remove Barriers**

Tessie looked on as Dorothy pointed to the first bullet. "The primary role of a leader is to paint a clear picture of success. Leaders need to be able to see beyond where they currently are to clearly articulate where they would like to be."

Dorothy moved to the second bullet. "Next, leaders need to be able to inspire others to move toward their visions of success. Simon Sinek discusses this in his landmark TED Talk, 'How Great Leaders Inspire Action.'"

Moving to the third bullet, Dorothy continued. "Finally, leaders remove barriers to achieving success." She put down the pen and looked directly at Tessie before continuing. "This is what leaders are called to do. Anything else isn't leadership. This is easy to lose sight of when there are pressures to meet deadlines or deliver revenue. When pressures increase, leaders are tempted to micromanage key situations, thinking they can save the day. Actually they could be robbing themselves and others of key learning opportunities for greater success in the long term." Dorothy looked over the page prior to moving on.

Moving down on the page, Dorothy drew a circle on the yellow pad and wrote the word *Actions* inside of it. "Tess, there are three elements every leader must master." Dorothy realized the yellow pad wouldn't be large enough to drive home the point she hoped to make, so she moved to a flip chart positioned in the corner of her office.

Dorothy redrew and labeled the circle prior to continuing her point. "Most people focus on leadership actions or behaviors. They start here because this is what they can see. They see leaders who they believe are successful, and they try to emulate their behaviors. They copy their dress, walk, key phrases, and so on. Some organizations use the same approach to identify management candidates. They find people who look the part, have executive presence or charisma, and so on." Dorothy gestured with her hands to demonstrate how far this element can go.

Dorothy drew a larger circle on the flip chart and began adding arrows to represent problems within the organization. "There's a problem with starting with actions and behaviors. When the real world sets in and arrows start flying, these leaders may not be able to think deeply, or they could lack credibility in their subject matter to galvanize others to solve complex problems."

LEADERSHIP RESIDUE

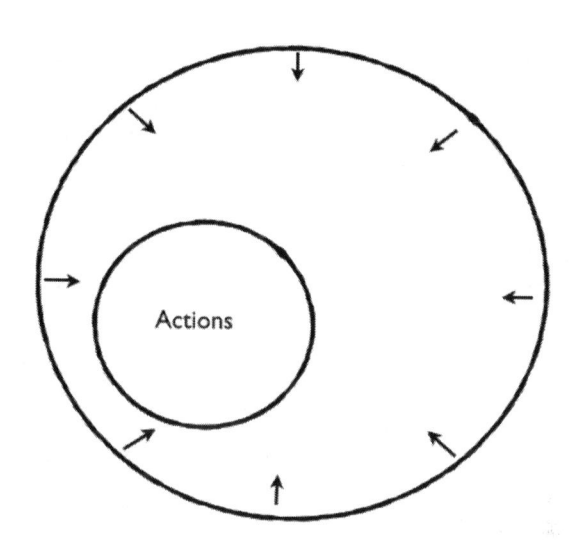

Dorothy continued. "So in the midst of real-world challenges, new leaders look quickly for the knowledge they lack to solve problems and build credibility. With no time to build broad knowledge, the best they can do is find problem-specific knowledge. Unfortunately, when new problems arise, they are unprepared to handle what they haven't seen before. These leaders repeat the tactical loop of learning and acting until enough problems have come across their desk to build a broad knowledge base." Dorothy drew a second circle, which she labeled *"Knowledge."* She added more arrows to represent the increasing pressure.

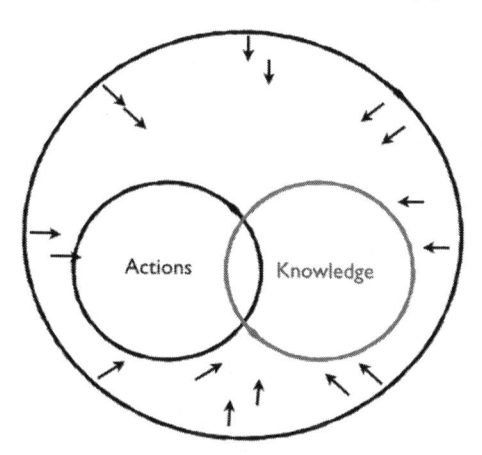

Dorothy continued. "Realizing borrowed actions and problem-specific knowledge aren't enough, new leaders read leadership books, attend seminars, or take a class or two on leadership. Somewhere along the way, they learn the importance of leaders having and communicating personal values. So they add value-based leadership to the mix, expecting this to solve their problems. All the while arrows continue to come." Dorothy drew another circle, which she labeled "*Values,*" and added more arrows.

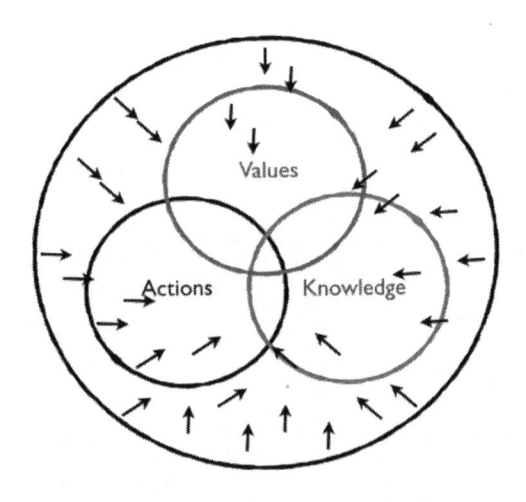

[Diagram: Three overlapping circles labeled "Values," "Actions," and "Knowledge" inside a larger circle, with arrows pointing inward from all sides.]

"They are right; values are important. However, under this kind of pressure, the most valuable thing a leader can do is solve the problem that created the mess. Unfortunately the leader could be the problem." Dorothy looked for cues Tessie was still following her logic.

Tessie's eyes were twice their normal size as she tried to play back what she had heard. "So every leader needs actions, knowledge, and values. This model has all three. Why is there still a problem?"

Dorothy smiled as she tore the page off of the flip-chart pad. "You've asked a brilliant question, Tess. The answer involves the priority the leader gives each element." Placing the first page on the table, Dorothy moved back to the flip chart. "This time we'll start with personal values." She drew a circle as she had done the first time.

Values

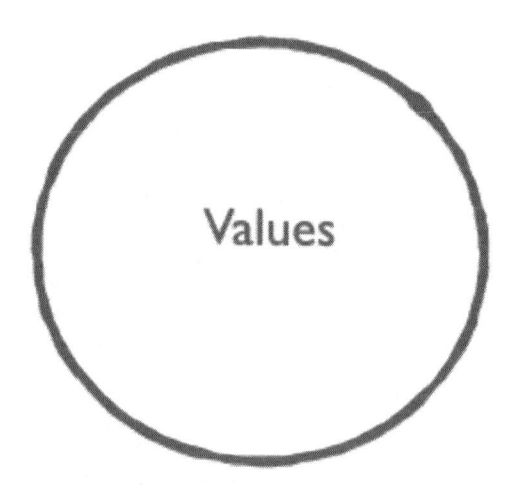

Dorothy continued. "Since these are personal, we don't have to wait for a leadership responsibility. Anyone can—and everyone should—answer five questions to uncover their personal values." She wrote down the questions.

1. Who are you?
2. What do you believe?
3. Why are you here?
4. Where are you going?
5. Who is going with you?

"Tess, this is quite simple, but it's by no means an easy task." Dorothy brushed her curls to the back of her ear.

Looking at Dorothy, Tessie asked, "Did you do this at the four-year university?"

Dorothy looked at the flip chart and shook her head. "Professors gave me all the tools I needed in school, but I was too worried about grades back then. In school I was too focused on trying to parrot back answers to impress someone else. There's no one to impress with this work. This is all about uncovering and documenting what you value as a person. Even if you never share this document, it would be a great reminder of who you aspire to be."

Tessie admitted being a bit lost. "I don't know if I could answer these questions."

Dorothy nodded in agreement. "As I said, this work is simple but not at all easy. It could take months or years for you get to what you truly value. One the hardest things people can do is be themselves instead of who they believe they are *supposed* to be.

"What about the other two circles, knowledge and actions?" Tessie asked.

Dorothy drew the two circles. Then she added arrows flowing from the values circle to each of the two new circles.

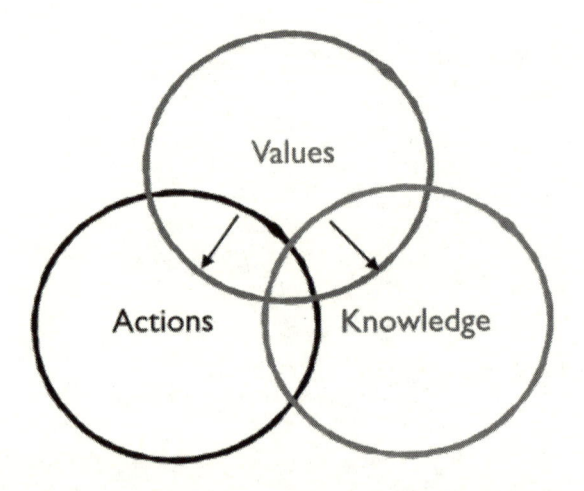

Diagram: three overlapping circles labeled Values, Actions, and Knowledge, with arrows from Values pointing down to Actions and Knowledge.

"Another great observation, Tess. When leaders understand and document their personal values first, the challenge moves to ensuring their knowledge and actions are consistent with the values they identified. The more values, actions, and knowledge align, the more obvious individuals become as leaders people are drawn to follow.

"Ultimately the aspiration is for total alignment. Ideally onlookers shouldn't be able to tell if they are viewing the leader's values, a demonstration of his or her knowledge, or the leader's normal behavior. For the leader, he or she is always living all three at once. The leader is just being him- or herself."

Dorothy wrote *"Effective Leadership"* on the top of the flip chart. "A person should do this work ahead of assuming leadership responsibility, prior to having to face the challenges of the real world. This is effective leadership even if you're leading only yourself. The challenge is more critical for people leaders, but the model still works for those who are not people leaders."

Effective Leadership

Values

Knowledge

Actions

Tessie squinted as she tried to understand the concept. "Why would it be important for me to do this work before becoming a leader? I may not want to lead people."

Dorothy answered Tessie's question. "By understanding your values, you can make career and life decisions based on what's important to you. Without a value-based foundation, someone may be tempted to take on a leadership role for the money, only to find he or she doesn't like what people leaders have to do. What's the value of making lots of money if your days will be filled with activities leaving you depressed and drained at the end of each day?"

Tessie gave an understanding smile. "So when all three are aligned is when a leader has residue."

Dorothy moved back toward the flip chart. "Almost, Tess, almost. Aligning values, knowledge, and actions is just effective leadership. At a minimum everyone deserves to have a leader with clearly articulated values and knowledge about his or her subject matter and who takes appropriate actions to move the organization closer to its mission. Residue comes when a leader's influence lingers to impact behavior after he or she is physically gone."

Tessie raised both hands as if surrendering. "I'm afraid I still don't understand the residue part."

Dorothy put down the marker and sat at the table next to Tessie. "Look at it this way. Have you ever had someone in your life who impacted you so much, you continue to think about him or her as you make decisions? It could be a teacher, a parent, or a mentor. It could be a friend, someone in a history book, or someone you have seen only from afar."

Tessie thought for a second. "You mean like 'what would Jesus do'?" She squinted again.

Dorothy tapped Tessie on the arm out of excitement. "Exactly! Jesus is a great example. None of the people living today who identify as being Christian have physically seen Jesus, yet they follow his principles, memorize his words, and try to emulate his behaviors. Some are even willing to die to advance what Jesus believed to be true. He has been gone for over two thousand years. I would say Jesus would be a great example of someone who had positive leadership residue." Dorothy walked back over to the flip chart to continue.

Tessie raised her hand slightly to ask another question. "Well, if a leader has mastered all three elements of leadership, what else is needed to create positive leadership residue?"

Dorothy drew all three circles again. "Very perceptive, Tess. There's a missing element we haven't discussed. The missing element is emotion. To have residue the effective leader has to create emotion. Emotion increases memory both positively and negatively. That's why it's easy for us to remember our first kiss, a make-believe tea party with our grandparents, achievement of a lifelong goal, or some other positive experience. Likewise, we can vividly remember our first heartbreak, the day a pet died, or some other painful experience. These experiences are all

LEADERSHIP RESIDUE

laden with emotion. The more intense the emotion, the more we tend to remember details of the event. We even make up additional details to further justify the emotions we felt."

Dorothy started labeling the overlaps of the circles on her flip chart. "A leader with negative residue would elicit negative emotions. These could be associated with you feeling controlled or having limited to no decision-making ability or employees being valued only for mindless execution. For some, working for this leader might be a vacation from having to think. For others, this leader could be a total nightmare."

[Venn diagram: three overlapping circles labeled "Values," "Actions," and "Knowledge." Labels with arrows: "Employee Compliance" points to the overlap of Values and Actions; "Centralized Decision-Making" points to the overlap of Values and Knowledge; "Employee Executes Only" points to the overlap of Actions and Knowledge.]

Tessie nodded. "I've worked in offices where I felt like this kind of tension. The manager never said anything mean, but somehow I got the message loud and clear. I couldn't wait to clock out each day."

Dorothy's smile appeared again. "In a pretty popular YouTube video, author and London Business School management professor Sumantra Ghoshal called this '*the smell of the place.*' You felt the emotional markers the leader created or allowed in the organization. The underlying message was that you were in a contract relationship. Additionally, your contract was renewed at the discretion of the leader or company."

Tessie raised questions to further her understanding. "Isn't that true, though? Doesn't the manager determine whether or not I keep my job? Why should he or she care about my emotions?"

Dorothy explained, "Well, you're right. The manager has a lot of influence over your employment. He or she is also key to how well you do your job based on the environment he or she creates. If the environment encourages compliance and constraint, you may never grow beyond being able to perform current tasks. As more complex issues arise, the manager must fly in like a superhero to make decisions and give direction for you to complete the task. Management is important, but it shouldn't be confused with leadership. Managers ensure people adhere to constraints in order to deliver a plan; leaders inspire people beyond constraints so they can do more than they previously imagined."

Dorothy changed a few of the labels on her flip chart. "A manager with positive leadership residue conjures positive emotions. Those emotions might be transparency, such as having clearly defined decision rights and full empowerment to act consistent with company values. This manager has given you the freedom to bring more of yourself to work. By feeling valued beyond your ability to execute current tasks, you may look for additional opportunities to help the mission succeed. You feel ownership in the organization's success. This manager can spend less time on day-to-day tasks and more time focused on higher-level strategies and complex problems that only he or she can address. You will forever approach issues with the residue of the leader's philosophy in mind. Sometimes the impact of his or her philosophy will even outlast your formal reporting relationship."

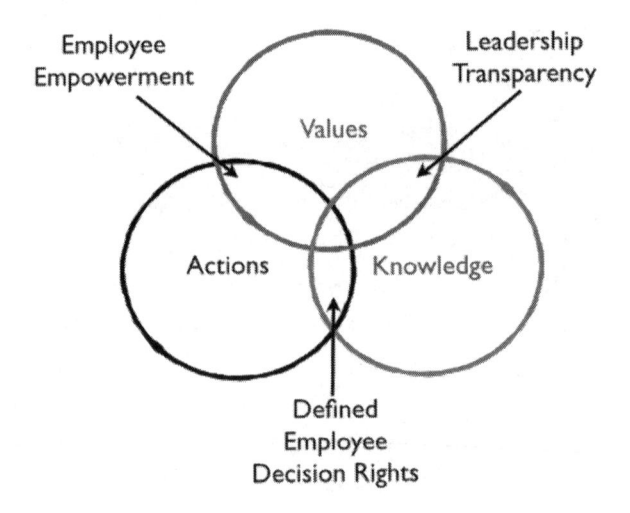

LEADERSHIP RESIDUE

Tessie walked over to the flip chart. "That's amazing. All you did was change the emotional markers on the flip chart, and I already feel better about working with this leader."

Dorothy tore the current sheet off the flip chart and placed it near the others on the table. "But you haven't heard the best part. Hand me the sheet we titled '*Effective Leadership.*'"

Tessie sorted through the sheets on the table.

Dorothy darkened the marker lines and added arrows to the chart and as she continued, "When all three leadership elements align and you add positive emotion, the organization adds to its protection against the real-world challenges. The emotion is like a force field of energy affecting everything they do. Issues still come; they just don't affect the people in the organization the same way. The people are more likely to remain loyal and focused on the mission."

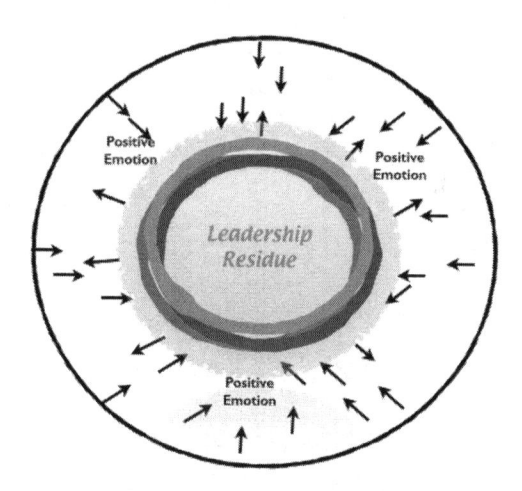

While studying Dorothy's flip-chart image, Tessie uttered a quote as if chanting Holy Scripture during a small church devotion. "People will forget what you say, people will forget what you do, but people will never forget how you made them feel."

Dorothy nodded her head. "Ah, number one hundred seventeen, Dr. Maya Angelou. You are absolutely correct." Dorothy commended Tessie with a nod for the well-placed reference.

"Yeah, I've been studying the list you gave me last month. Number one hundred seventeen was one of my favorites. Where did you get this list from, anyway?" Tessie opened her notebook and pulled out the stapled sheets titled *"Beans Wall Quotes."*

Dorothy smiled as she looked over the list of quotes.

Tessie returned her attention back to the flip chart. "But if leaders can't make people follow, how can they make them have a positive emotion?"

Dorothy folded her arms as she walked toward Tessie and the flip chart. "Well, Tess, the honest answer is they can't. Leaders can't *make* people do anything. So much of someone's emotion has to do with what's happening in their own brain—the amygdala part of the brain, to be exact. This is why two people can see the same event differently. Their amygdalae assign emotional tags to give the event meaning. Those emotional tags are influenced by their moods, surroundings, and a host of other things the leader can't possibly know about. When leaders give up the notion they can *make* people deliver results, act a certain way, or even feel a certain way, it frees everyone."

Tessie squinted and shook her head slightly as if still not fully grasping. "So then what's the point?"

Dorothy touched Tessie on the arm gently. "Remember what we said were the three things leaders are called to do?"

Tessie looked at her notes before responding. "Leaders create a picture of success, inspire action, and remove barriers."

Dorothy tapped the table three times quickly. "That's right. Nowhere in the job description does it say anything about *making* people follow. A leader *inspires* by appealing to everyone's desire for authenticity. Even if the follower doesn't understand fully, he or she wants to have confidence the leader is committed to everyone's success—not just his or her own."

Tessie nodded slowly as Dorothy continued. "When you see politicians, business leaders, or other leaders for the first time, do you always know what they're talking about?"

Tessie thought for a minute. "To think about it, no. Mostly I just listen to how they speak, I look at how they're dressed, and I watch how they interact with people."

Dorothy smiled widely as she nodded her head. "Everyone does the same thing the first time they meet someone. This visual evaluation goes into overdrive when you meet a possible leader. We're trying to determine if we should give the leader our allegiance, our discretionary resources. Can this leader be trusted?

Dorothy continued. "There's a lot of research on how the brain works and how perception contributes to building trust. Your body uses microexpressions to reconcile inconsistency between your words and your thoughts. Most microexpressions occur in the eye region. Detection by others occurs subconsciously. This is why people whose livelihoods depend on their ability to mislead, like professional poker players, wear sunglasses or hats to shade their eyes."

Tessie leaned forward to ask her next question. "So what do microexpressions have to do with leadership?"

Dorothy smiled before continuing. "By reading microexpressions, people can determine if their leader believes in his or her own words and actions. If there's inconsistency, people may not fully commit. In other words, if the leader doesn't believe in the mission, even if he or she tries, he or she can't hide it. Microexpressions send subconscious messages to others, indicating there's no need for followers to believe. Even if followers can't articulate what they see, their gut tells them *something's wrong*. Frequent inconsistency will cause people to lose confidence in the leader. Frequent inconsistency with multiple leaders in the same organization will cause people to lose confidence in the organization itself."

Dorothy tucked her curls behind her right ear and continued. "The opposite is also true. If a leader consistently projects microexpressions indicating he or she truly and passionately believes what he or she is doing, others will pick up on them and seek opportunities to align with that leader's cause, continue his or her mission, and even invest discretionary time or resources to help ensure success."

Tessie's puzzled look lightened slightly before Dorothy continued. "Tess, it's kind of like a *BS meter*. Can't you tell when a salesperson or someone else is trying to *BS* you? Well, the same is true for leaders. It is probably even truer for leaders you get to see in a variety of situations over time."

Dorothy walked back to her desk and sat in her chair. "To be a leader with positive residue, you need values you believe in, relevant knowledge, behavior consistent with beliefs and knowledge, and authentic emotions to connect with people without setting off their BS meters."

Tessie nodded her head while smiling broadly. She commented again without moving her eyes from the flip chart. "I think I get it now. A leader who truly believes in his or her mission will attract people who connect with the leader's message and mission. Authentic positive emotions achieve residue. The leader must truly believe in what he or she is doing because microexpressions make authenticity impossible to fake."

Dorothy smiled without saying a word.

Tessie turned her gaze from the flip chart to Dorothy. "Ma'am, if you didn't get this in school, how did you learn about leadership residue?"

Dorothy looked at the sheet of quotes Tessie had tossed on the table earlier, leaned back in her chair, and smiled. "Let's just say I have a lot of residue from an emotional college experience involving friends, a wicked professor, a wizard, and a small coffee shop. Although I'm not in Kansas anymore, my memories help guide the leader I'm trying to become."

Dorothy folded the flip-chart sheets and handed them to Tessie. "Well, I guess we're out of time for today. Let me know if I can help you at all between now and when we meet again."

Dorothy walked Tessie to the door, where they exchanged hugs and good-byes. Returning to her desk, Dorothy turned to the window, reflecting on the conversation with Tessie and her own journey from

Kansas to AU to WB Tech Solutions to her current role at E. Mill Corp. She whispered to herself, "I guess there was something about the beans after all."

The End

PART 5
TOOLS AND RESOURCES

Beans Wall Quotes #32: "Knowing yourself is the beginning of all wisdom." — Aristotle

DOROTHY'S SUBMISSION

"All I Know about Leadership, I Learned from The Wizard of Oz*"*

1. **The Wizard of Oz:** There is no wizard behind the curtain. At best, there are smart people who hope you will never learn of their insecurities or failures. They are all well-meaning but insecure. A leader must not depend on someone to arrive with all the answers.
2. **The Lion:** Leaders need courage to do the right thing, regardless of whether it is convenient or not. It doesn't take courage to do what is convenient. True leaders make decisions based on an internal compass of integrity.
3. **Dorothy:** Everyone feels lost from time to time, even leaders. The key is to not give up. Continue to look for solutions and find a network of like-minded, optimistic people to join your quest.
4. **The Scarecrow:** Those who would have you think you have no brain only fear they wouldn't be able to control your thinking. Leaders know how to influence outcomes regardless of recognition or credit.
5. **Toto:** Stick with your friends, and find the fun in everything. Leaders understand everything is about perspective. There is a silver lining for those who choose to look.
6. **Auntie Em:** Stay in touch with people who know the real you. Even if they aren't physically around, their memories can keep you grounded through all the accolades and criticism.
7. **The Tin Man:** Leaders must have a heart when it comes to the personal lives, goals, and ambitions of others. This is beyond th**e bottom**

line and is at the core of authenticity. Others know when you are playing a part and when you care.
8. **The Good Witch:** Mentors and coaches are always there to help you believe in yourself, even if only as a reminder of lessons learned in your past. Their job isn't necessarily to provide answers but to provide space to learn.
9. **The Wicked Witch:** Those who wish you ill are usually guided by fear. Dangers may be real but not insurmountable. Apply courage, brains, and your network to the success of the mission. More than anything, believe—despite your limitations— you are more than enough to succeed.

PROFESSOR WICCO'S ASSIGNED READING LIST

1. *Start with Why* by Simon Sinek
2. *Now Discover Your Strengths* by Marcus Buckingham and Donald Clifton
3. *HBR's 10 Must Reads on Leadership* compiled by *Harvard Business Review*
4. *5 Choices of Extraordinary Productivity* by Franklin Covey
5. *Fierce Conversations* by Susan Scott
6. *The Articulate Executive* by Granville Toogood
7. *Situational Leadership II* by Ken Blanchard
8. *Becoming a Leader-Coach* by Johan Naude and Florence Plessier
9. *The Presentation Secrets of Steve Jobs* by Carmine Gallo
10. *Smell of the Place* (YouTube video) by Sumantra Ghoshal
11. *Oh, the Places You'll Go* by Dr. Seuss
12. *The 21 Indispensable Qualities of a Leader* by John C. Maxwell
13. *Jesus CEO* by Laurie Beth Jones
14. *Change the World* by Robert Quinn
15. *Be, Know, Do* by Frances Hesselbein
16. *A User's Guide to the Brain* by John J. Ratey, MD (page 186)
17. *Trust and Trustworthiness* by Russell Hardin
18. *Leading Change* by John P. Kotter
19. *Outliers* by Malcolm Gladwell

20. *The Art of War for Executives* by Donald G. Krause
21. *Trombone Player Wanted* by Marcus Buckingham
22. *The Five Dysfunctions of a Team* by Patrick Lencioni
23. *Good to Great* by Jim Collins

CRAFTING DOROTHY'S LEADERSHIP PLATFORM

1. **Who are YOU?**
   - What comes easy for you; but seemingly not to others?
   - Things you are good at and energized while completing the task?

2. **What do YOU believe?**
   - What have you learned about life and the world?
   - What beliefs do you hold that you cannot be convinced otherwise?

3. **Why are YOU here?**
   - How could your strengths, beliefs, passions and experiences benefit the world or others?

4. **Where are YOU going?**
   - What is your vision of what the world COULD be?

5. **Who is going with YOU?**
   - How can you identify people who can help achieve your vision or benefit from your mentorship?

CRAFTING DOROTHY'S LEADERSHIP RESIDUE PLAN

Values: What do you believe to be true?
1. What is important to you?
2. What are you good at doing? Do you enjoy it?
3. What are you here to accomplish?

Knowledge: What information do you need to gain?
1. How do you execute key tasks?
2. How will you identify and relate with key people?
3. What do you understand about navigating the environment?

Actions/Behaviors: What do you need to be able to do?
1. How must you behave to deliver critical objectives?
2. What behavior will influence others to action?
3. How much change is needed to meet required actions and behaviors?

Emotion: Do you generate positive or negative emotions for others?
1. Why is it important that you live the values you profess?
2. What do you want to inspire people to feel, say, or do?
3. What residue would you like to leave for others?
4. Can anyone tell what you are passionate about?

PART 6
REAL LIFE EXAMPLES OF LEADERSHIP RESIDUE

Beans Wall Quote #131: "The task of leadership is not to put greatness into humanity, but to elicit it, for the greatness is already there." — John Buchan

NO FICTION HERE

Leadership in every field carries responsibility. All leaders derive personal inspiration from people in their pasts. As you read the following true leadership-residue stories from senior executives, educators, lawyers and nonprofit leaders honoring those who have inspired them, consider your personal story. Who has invested in you? In small or significant ways, who do you consider when making decisions? More importantly, who is your residue influencing? Who might be watching you for lessons on how to lead others? All leaders leave residue. Be purposeful to ensure your leadership residue is positive. You can honor those who have inspired you by sharing your story at www.Leadership-Residue.com.

1. Anna Crosslin—President & CEO, International Institute of St. Louis:

While I have been inspired to lead by numerous people during my lengthy career, two individuals stand out. The first is my mother; the second is my first full-time boss, a university professor.

My mom is a Japanese immigrant who arrived in America speaking no English and with health problems. My dad, a linguist with the US Air Force, was her lifeline. Five years later, she was a widow with very young children. There ensued thirty-five years of frequently excruciatingly hard work for her. She owned and operated a series of restaurants to put food on the table for her four children and later to ensure we could attend college. As the oldest of the children, my role was to take care of myself, help mom at the restaurant, and also care for my younger siblings.

Stanley, my first real boss, was also an entrepreneur, albeit in a university setting. In the period following World War II, he had entered the field of Chinese studies, quite a stretch for a young Jewish male from the Bronx. He was hired by Washington University in 1953, I believe. He went on to found the Department of Chinese & Japanese, the Asian Studies Program, the East Asia Library, and nearly all things Asian at the university and in St. Louis.

By the time I arrived to serve as his assistant fifteen years later, Stanley was frequently traveling nationally and internationally. So he basically left me to "mind the shop" (i.e., the Office of International Studies, which he also founded). Here I was, a recent graduate of twenty-one, arranging lunches for foreign dignitaries and pulling together faculty groups for grants and projects. I stayed with Stanley for six years and then moved to the International Institute of St. Louis, where I remain today.

It is easy to see that I have been inspired by great leaders, leaders who were willing to yield control and who expressed confidence that others could complete tasks, perhaps differently but acceptably. So I approach the role of being a leader today by trying to reflect the attributes that I feel are valuable to model. Among others, those are the value of thinking strategically, being entrepreneurial, acting inclusively, and above all, persevering and being resilient.

2. Bruce Shead—Marketing Manager, Bemis Company, Inc.:

I had a coworker who was very meticulous in how he worked, detailed in his space of responsibility, and more than anything, true to himself with strong self-belief. His relationship with other coworkers in conversation and working agendas never varied based on the level or title of the individual. The corporate game to him did not matter, and he shared a story of his infant stage in corporate America that really has now become part of my Leadership Residue.

He told me of the time when he was very disciplined in following the direction of his past managers—not just in his task on the job but also in some of those unspoken corporate rules. His objectives exceeded expectations, and his ratings were stellar. However, even with all these accomplishments, he still found himself laid off because of a company restructure.

That is when he made up in his mind that he was going to continue to excel in his next job on own his terms, redefining his own corporate etiquette.

His approach to both his professional and personal life mantra is, "I am my own cause." For me it really left a peaceful Leadership Residue because it was not a selfish position but one that inspired me to be the best to myself in order to be the very best to others. That freed me from the bureaucracy of people who want to emulate others in chase of a dream without knowing themselves. That residue allowed me to see things for what they are and understand that you are only as good as you believe you are.

Titles in the workforce are nothing more than that: a title. I am defined by who I am versus the title given to me by an organization. This has allowed me to be more confident in my approach and freed me from some of the boundaries I use to place on myself. So when I think of Leadership Residue, I am glad that I have had a positive experience that serves as a filter to continuously support me while limiting the toxicity around me.

3. KP Westmoreland—Inspirational Communicator, Author, CEO, Westmoreland Ministries:

Yesterday, a young man came up to me and told me about a time (when he was in junior high) that I presented him with an award at a camp. Now, nearly twenty years later, he's a grown man and has a wife and children. Yet, he still remembers an event from his childhood. He recalled the "Good Attitude" award he received from me years before as if it were last week. I'm reminded of what an impact we can have on people.

Today, we have an opportunity to make a lasting impact on others that might mean more to them than we could ever imagine. It doesn't take much. Maybe a smile, an encouraging comment, or a simple acknowledgment of their great value. We never know what impact we are having on people that might be remembered by them for years to come. Today, we will be making an impact that will affect someone greatly for years to come. I pray that we make it a positive impact that glorifies God and allows the person to see God's love and the great value they have in God's sight.

Today, you will impact someone. I hope that twenty years from now you get to hear from them how meaningful your impact was upon them and their life. God bless!

4. Regis Bingham—Chief Executive Officer, Business Marketing Enterprises:

I have had two employers who I never considered to be bosses. They were my mentors. I stay in contact with them to this day, even though I have not worked with them in over nine years. One thing that has always impressed me about their leadership styles is their ability to garner the loyalty of their employees. They taught me a lot about management. The most important Leadership Residue that has dripped all over me is that I should constantly try to work myself out of a job. They stressed the importance of training people to do your job better than you can do the job. I can still hear them say, "Regis, you are working too hard. The more you do, the worse they will get. Train them to do what you do." That is my Leadership Residue story.

5. Bill Dougherty—Sales Leader and Entrepreneur:

I remember one manager, Ken, at Coca-Cola, who helped shape my outlook on risk. I was concerned about accepting a position as a bottler account manager. Ken seemed to sense my concern, but also reminded me of obstacles I had previously overcome in my current position. Ken then reflected on situations from his past where he accomplished things that had been previously thought impossible or at least improbable. It was the genuine love of the experience, reflected both in Ken's eyes and in the tone of his voice, that convinced me that life lived for security was not as fulfilling as life lived to make a difference. I knew that, to make a difference, you must accept the risk that comes from being an agent of change, but Ken showed me you could also enjoy it. This risk paid off, and I've continued to accept risks, including turning around another underperforming market, adopting two children from a foreign country, and starting my own business. I'll always be thankful to Ken for making life an adventure.

LEADERSHIP RESIDUE

6. Anthony Gray—Partner, Johnson Gray LLC:

In the legal profession, and when it comes to legal analysis, I typically consult a good friend of mine by the name of Rufus J. Tate Jr. (attorney at law). He is truly the initial source and inspiration of any decision that I make in a legal context. I totally admire his analytical skills and his thought processes. Very few people elaborate like Rufus when simply posed with a question. He offers more than just a quick answer. For that, I truly value and admire him.

Leaders are more than just great people of action. Their words must be full of substance, which tends to resolve problems faced either by themselves or by others. That's something indicative of Rufus. And yes, we have this trait in common.

7. Willie Diefenbach-Jones—Distributor, SendOutCards:

One of the many people who has had a mega-influence on me is my second-grade teacher. She was very fit and started each day in our classroom leading us in exercises. These were light exercises, not heavy cardio. They were to get the body warmed up so that we could open our minds to learning and eliminate any sluggish feelings that we might have. To this day, I sometimes will stand at my desk and do some light exercises to shake a sluggish feeling. She taught a great habit, and I think of her often.

The other thing that she taught was that the classroom faced south and that she stood on the south. She taught us to look at her, and to the left was east, where the sun rose, and to the right was west. When I am direction challenged, I often ground myself with second grade and facing the teacher, who was on the south side. Then I know left is east and right is west. The funny thing about that is many of my second-grade friends still relate to that exercise. It's the simple things that we remember.

8. George Bingham—Executive Producer, In the Community with George Bingham Television Show:

Mr. C. L. Seaton was affectionately known as "Prof." As home economics was taught to the girls, Prof taught agriculture to the boys at the now-defunct Eliza Miller High School in West Helena, Arkansas. He held a master's degree from the Tuskegee Institute founded by Booker

T. Washington. If you meet any of the hundreds of boys he taught, they will tell you exactly what I am going to tell you. I know because I am the president of the school's alumni association.

At an all-school reunion, there was an impromptu gathering of boys from class years 1954 to 1970. Prof was the topic of a very emotional conversation, and we all called ourselves "Prof's boys." Some proofs of Prof's "teaching residue" are: David L. Evans, an admissions officer at Harvard University; Thomas L. Wright, an eye surgeon; Larry L. Williams, an attorney in Los Angles, California; and countless bank vice presidents, college professors, and dentists who, if asked about their inspiration, would point to Prof.

Prof would insist on your learning public speaking and parliamentary procedures, but most of all, he never failed to tell us how each class was going to benefit us in real life. He taught by opportunity. If you made a mistake, he would say, "It ain't bad if you don't know. What's bad is when you don't know and don't know that you don't know."

When you walked into his physical classroom, there was a picture of a turtle hanging on the wall. He never mentioned it. Instead, he waited all year, if he had to, until inevitably some wise-A student would ask, "Hey Prof, what's the picture of that turtle up there for?" I must admit, one year I was guilty of being the wise-A student. You could hear "ahh Bingham" from the older boys. He said, "Little Bingham, I'm glad you asked," and following was nearly an hour lecture on the turtle. Summarized, it went:

> That turtle represents your success or failure in life. You see a turtle gets nowhere until he sticks out his neck, which means you must not be afraid to take a risk. He can't move as long as his neck is tucked safely in his shell. If a turtle wants to cross the street bad enough, he must take the risk of getting hit by a car—he must take the risk and stick out his neck. You'll leave home one day and be on your own; always remember you can't always know: sometimes you just have to chance it. The turtle

tells you another thing about life. You see how slow the turtle moves? Your success or failure comes the same way: very slowly.

The residue of Prof's lesson is that I have always had pictures of turtles in my home and car. I taught this lesson to Galen and his brother and sister. But even more, today I'm telling you. I'll bet you'll be telling someone tomorrow. When you tell the turtle story, it's alright to say, "Prof said."

9. Ronald J. Moore—Business Executive:

Early in my managerial career, I was given the opportunity to turn around a market where my company had low share. I inherited a manager and hired a team full of energetic, young, smart, hard-charging associates with the potential to fast track through the organization. Shortly after hiring the associates, I realized the manager that I had inherited did not have the required sales skill, knowledge, and leadership ability to lead these new associates. The manager was a very nice person with great intentions. However, she had been miscast. I knew that she would quickly lose the respect of the team that I had just hired. It was my first managerial position in the company, and I was reluctant to replace the manager so quickly.

My region vice president realized my personal dilemma. He told me that sometimes the decisions that are the best decisions for people are the hardest to make. Sometimes you need to help people find their way, and it might be painful initially, but they will ultimately be happier. I had a long conversation with the person, placed her on probation, and ultimately severed her from the company. It was a very difficult conversation.

Two years later, she called and personally thanked me. She stated that she was never happy in the position and was always stressed and tense. After leaving the company, she followed her love of cooking and went to culinary school. She was so happy not having all the stress. She mentioned she would have never done that on her own if it hadn't been for our conversation. I realized that being a leader sometimes requires you to make unpopular decisions that force people to find their calling. If I had not forced her to find a new position and backfilled her with what became an excellent leader, she would have been miserable, the new associates would have been miserable, and a promising young leader may not have been placed in a position to shine.

10. Greg Strauss—SVP of Specialty Products, AB Mauri North America:

I have worked for many individuals during the past twenty-four years—some good and some not so good. However, I have learned something from each of them; in some cases it was actually how *not* to lead and manage people. What my better managers have taught me are the following ten keys to successful leadership:

1. Be passionate about your company, your customers, and the industry you serve.
2. Lead by example.
3. Demonstrate empathy. (Even if the manager cannot perform the same technical functions as well as the direct reports, he or she should fully understand what they do and be seen as putting forth the same or a greater effort than his or her employees.)
4. Share the company vision, and provide clear direction as it relates to your department.
5. Listen to your direct reports.
6. Ensure that direct reports are properly trained, and then empower them to make decisions.
7. Always act with integrity.
8. Be consistent.
9. Constantly improve.
10. Hire the right person for the job.

These sound easy, but I have only seen a precious few be able to fully embody these successful traits. (By the way, I myself am still working at them. I learn something new every single day.)

11. Stephen O'Hara—Retired CEO of Rawlings Sporting Goods and Angelica Corporation; Current Board Member of three companies, Author and Investor:

I have three stories I would like to tell:

First: When I was a freshman in high school, I did not make the varsity teams, so I was playing Catholic Youth Organization (CYO) basketball. My CYO coach, Don Doucette, was committed to helping me get better and make the varsity team at school, which I did my junior year. Forty-five years later, I remember one key lesson above all others.

In a practice scrimmage, I was playing point guard, and I threw a pass underneath to our center that hit him in the hands and rolled out of bounds. Coach blew the whistle, stopped play, and yelled at me for throwing the pass. I responded defensively, saying, "Coach, I hit him in the hands. What else do you want me to do?"

Coach responded, "Your job is not to make a pass you feel great about. Your job is to give him a pass he can handle so he scores! Know your teammates. Your center doesn't have the same hands as a guard—he needs a different, better pass."

Throughout my career I have used this story with managers who are responsible for a project and claim some failure is not their fault. If you have the ball in your hands, it is your responsibility and your fault if we lose the ball.

Second: Early in my career at Procter & Gamble, I succeeded because I would fight through obstacles to get things done. This led to rapid promotions and early success in my career. Although blowing through walls might offend some people, since promotions followed I came to believe that achieving the goal was all that mattered.

After leaving P&G for my first vice-president title at Boston Whaler, my new boss, Joe Lawler, called me into his office and let me know that my style was unacceptable. He noted that I was now senior management and that how I got things done was as important as what I got done. Achieving a goal but creating a bad environment was not appropriate.

Fortunately, my parents had raised me to understand that winning the game "the right way" was important, so there was still some fertile ground on which Joe's message could fall. I changed, and Joe's message has been a huge part of the future successes I achieved.

Thirdly: In my first supervisory job at P&G, I had an extremely bright young woman working for me. She would regularly make excellent points in our discussions and lead us to better ideas and plans. However, when we would go up the ladder with plans she would develop, she would sit mute or answer meekly when my boss or other senior managers challenged the plans, even when she knew the answer or was correct.

I was having difficulty changing this behavior, and her promising career was in jeopardy, when I decided to try something. I "ordered" her to disagree at least twice in any meeting with my boss. I told her I didn't care if the sun was out and he said it was a beautiful day, I expected her to argue and say it was very humid and would probably rain. If it was dark out, I expected her to say how bright and sunny it was. She was to disagree at least twice, or her tenure with me would be in jeopardy. Correctly, she started disagreeing on better issues than sunshine or rain. She gained confidence, and years later her father thanked me for it, although we joked that we had let loose a monster.

The lesson was simple for me. I not only had to tell my subordinates what they needed to do to improve but had to give them concrete action steps that could change the poor habit.

12. Luke Bobo, PhD—Curriculum Director/Resident Theologian, Biblical Business Training:

"Tom," who is deceased, was the former CEO of a major securities business in St. Louis. I had the pleasure of interviewing this leader at his home. He quickly stated his priorities: clients first, employees second, and company third. In other words, his focus was not on making a profit or lining his pocket; rather, his focus was on faithful practice of the Golden Rule. For he believed that if you treated clients and employees like you want to be treated, then they would remain loyal. He was emphatic in that; he said, "I didn't preach it, but I lived it out."

Tom purposely kept his salary and other upper managers' salaries modest. Employees engaged in profit sharing and were given the option to participate in a stock option program. Because Tom lived out biblical principles before his employees and clients and made certain his management staff treated employees and clients with respect and dignity, Tom enjoyed record growth in this industry. Tom, who was appointed CEO in the mid-1960s, retired in 2001 and continued to get boxes of cards from employees until his death; many of these employees he never met in person, but they wished him well and expressed their heartfelt thanks.

My encounter with this leader was rather quite brief; however, I learned two valuable leadership lessons. One, it is because of Tom that I strive and endeavor to practice the Golden Rule to those in management and to those who report to me. And two, I am black and Tom was white; however, good leadership principles transcend race, class, creed, culture, or ethnicity.

13. Leonard Vines—Attorney, Greensfelder, Hemker & Gale, PC:

As a young lawyer, one of my mentors, a senior partner at the firm, taught me a valuable lesson. One of his clients was trying get zoning approval to build an office park. After spending a great deal of time, money, and effort, the client's zoning application was denied, and he had to scrap his plans for the development. Sensing how devastating the defeat must have been, I commented to my mentor, "Well, I guess that's the end of this project. How can your client handle the disappointment?"

In an optimistic tone, my mentor replied, "Our client has suffered many set-backs before. Whenever he hits a brick wall, he just picks himself up, turns around, and takes a different direction." As my mentor predicted, the client found another piece of property, and about a year later, his office park became a reality. I learned that successful people don't get discouraged when they face adversity; they keep going and don't let setbacks keep them down.

14. Dr. J. Russell Garris, PhD—Educator:

Words from my father: I do not remember how old I was or the context in which it was said: "Son all you have is your word, and when that is gone you have nothing." Dad was a blue-collar worker who said, "I don't want you to have to break your back making a living—I want you to use your brain." Implicit in that was, "I want you to respect everyone—no matter what you do, give it your best."

While I worked hard and was able to obtain several advanced degrees, I was never the brightest student in the class, but no one worked harder than I did to successfully complete the programs; I subscribed to the view that from those to whom much has been given much in turn is expected. This has always been my guide since I started work as a professional, whether as a superintendent, division head, supervisor, underling, or mentor. Those who have worked for or with me know that if Russ says something, then that is what he is going to do, what he will work toward, what he really believes. While my tenure in positions at times has not had the longevity I would have liked, there was always another job/advancement on the horizon, and they were made possible my former "leaders," who said to prospective employers, "If you want someone at your back who you can trust and respect—he is the one you want to fill the position."

Words from Dr. Frank Yulo: These came at a time when I was heading a desegregation project during the seventies—a very tense and emotional time, with intermittent threats of bodily harm. I always tried to be the voice of reason and rationality, with views toward the future. I was not a rabble-rouser and really questioned whether that was an approach I should adopt, as those were the persons who others appeared to listened to.

I shared this with Dr. Yulo, who was my supervisor and mentor, and his response was, "Russ, you have gotten to where you are by being the person that you are—if you change, you will not know what to do, and those around you will not know how to respond." As I reflect back, he was so right—those of other ethnicities were not afraid to approach me and ask really troubling but sincere questions that they were confronted with or dealing with. I am certain our interactions and exchanges had positive outcomes as they interacted with others.

Words from my mom: I am not certain of the words or deeds, but they resulted in my having a conscience and a sense of right and wrong—these came back at a crucial time in my youth.

There was a time in my youth when I really thought I could be a thug and had started to do some thuggish things, but in the recesses of my mind, there was this thought: Would you want someone to do this to a member of your family? If I did not want it done to a member of my family, I did not do it. There is no doubt in my mind that that was my mother talking to me.

15. Joe Ambrose—Regional President, First Bank, St. Louis, Missouri:

Like many others, I have picked up on the leadership styles of many throughout my career. The two people that have influenced me the greatest in my banking career were my first boss and my most recent boss.

My first job out of college was as a bank examiner with the Federal Deposit Insurance Corporation. I had the privilege of working for a manager, Ron, whose motto was "work hard, play harder." I didn't realize it at the time, but that attitude developed both a strong individual work ethic and an equally strong sense of team building. The FDIC held numerous training seminars for bank regulatory staff from across the country. Ron was the lead instructor for both the technical bank topics as well as the leadership training, so I had the best upbringing on a daily basis in all aspects that one could receive!

I worked for my most recent boss, Terry, for ten years. Early on, I picked up on his style taking the emotion out of business decisions. It was along the lines of *The Godfather*: "It's business, not personal." This isn't to ignore the human aspect of decisions, but I have found it easier to communicate expectations and give feedback when they are clearly stated in that manner. This works well when I am creating the right environment for all to do the best they can do. Everyone is held to the same standard of performance, which brings out the best in them.

So how does all this translate into my leadership style? I played and coached ice hockey for over forty years and view myself as a player-coach.

Most times I find it best to send out the right player and let them perform. At other times, I have to hop off the bench and show my teammates how to get it done. The obvious goal is to win the game, but that is accomplished by an all-out effort every time you touch the ice; the puck always seems to be on the stick of the player working the hardest.

16. Deputy Fire Chief Charles E. Coyle Sr.—Fire Marshal, St. Louis Fire Department:

I joined the St. Louis Fire Department in 1978 while still a twenty-one-year-old college student. It was at this early stage in my career that I had the fortunate opportunity of coming into contact with Assistant Fire Chief Preston Bouie. Chief Bouie was the first African American manager in the department's one-hundred-plus year history, and he quickly continued to rise through the ranks to second in command within the department.

During the late 1970s and the 1980s, the department was going through a complete overhaul from the mandates of the federal courts relating to equal rights and affirmative action, as were many departments throughout the country. These changes were at times volatile, and it was always challenging for management to adequately move the department forward. Chief Bouie, who was truly an effective manager, was an even greater leader. To witness how he addressed the day-to-day problems within the department (which other mangers seem to struggle with) and how employees on both sides of an issue believed that he had their and the department's best interests in mind when addressing these tasks or problems was like a carrot dangling in the sky for me. I wanted that. At the time I didn't know what it was, but I knew that I wanted it.

I watched how he carried himself, followed all decisions that he made, and wanted to know his thinking process in making those decisions, and I listened to every word he said. The effect he had on me and the other firefighters around me was one that I wanted to have on others.

Chief Bouie's office was located in city hall, which was three blocks from the fire station that I worked in. His response vehicle was always

LEADERSHIP RESIDUE

parked in my fire station. The process that was used is that he would drive his vehicle to the fire station in the morning and pick up a firefighter to ride with him to city hall, and that firefighter would bring his vehicle back to the fire station. If he needed his vehicle during the day or at the end of the day, a firefighter would pick him up, or he sometimes walked to the fire station. This process became my training opportunity. I would make sure that I was at the front of the fire station each morning, waiting for him to arrive, and make sure I was near the phone at the end of the day. This three-block ride was where I planned to find out what he had and how I could get it as well.

At the start of each day, I would think about the questions that I would ask him. Not only would I think of the questions but also how the questions should be worded to allow him the best opportunity to elaborate. Because I only had three blocks, timing and planning were critical. I would make sure I said good morning and awaited his response before entering the car, and since no professional firefighter would move a vehicle until his seat belt was fastened, I would ask my question either before I fastened or while I was fastening my seat belt. I would then sit back and listen. My only words (if not asked a question) would be, as he would exit the vehicle, "Thank you, Chief, and have great day." As time passed, he would spend more and more time speaking with me about leadership; he gave me his personal contact information in case I had any additional questions, which I always did.

Once I became a supervisor and then a manager, my focus remained on striving to be an excellent leader, still a work in progress. I read every book I could find and took classes as well, but more importantly, within my professional career, I've been influenced by a number of good leaders within my organization who created their own individual stories. Other than my mother, my personal leadership influence came from my uncle, James Harvey, whose presence defined character, integrity, and a genuine concern for others. Just listening to him inspired me.

As I reflect back to the 1990s and the first team of potential leaders that I mentored professionally (and in some cases about their personal lives), I recall just how hungry they were to learn, the conversations and the questions we shared, and the problems or concerns that we worked through to assist them, which enhanced my growth as a leader and mentor. Today all of them are leaders in their own right and are mentoring others. Out of this team, almost all of them are supervisors or managers; two head employee organizations, and two are pastors with successful churches. I still mentor them today, and we still enjoy sharing with each other the new and important areas of leadership that we are continually learning.

What truly brings me joy is having conversations with the potential leaders that the leaders that I have mentored are now mentoring. Hearing them speak of having the courage to do what they know is right no matter how difficult, finding the opportunity in problems, building trust in their teams, and protecting their integrity at all cost—these are many of the same conversations I had with their mentors.

Currently, as a top level manager, it takes more for me these days to feel the pulse of my team, and in some cases I am the last to know of a problem because of the layers of supervision between some team members and me. And with new and younger potential leaders within my team, it requires me to spend more time with the team in order to build the trust that is needed, as well as continuing to evaluate and improve my leadership skills while remaining focused on the needs of the team.

As I think of the leaders and potential leaders that I mentor today, I often think back to that three-block ride with Chief Bouie and the Leadership Residue that he left with me, which allows me the opportunity to leave Leadership Residue with others.

17. Na'im Madyun, PhD—Associate Dean of Undergraduate, Diversity and International Programs:

I read an article once on leadership development. In the article, it suggested that introverted individuals often become great leaders after they are told or pushed to lead. The reason the prodding increases the impact of their leadership is because the introverted individual spends time trying to reflexively examine his or her own skills and applying them to leadership. I share this because there are three important components of leadership I have learned from those I've mentored and those that I have led that the encouraged introvert also tends to engage in before assuming leadership.

The first is the importance of being true to who you are. It's difficult to consistently follow inconsistency. A leader who spends more time being true to an external audience more than he or she is true to an internal one will eventually have no audience or following at all.

The second component is symbiotic with the first. There must be a natural, unconditional passion behind the work that one consciously aligns with their true self. A leader should be driven by energy that comes naturally. Any writings, facts, references, and comments related to the work should refuel the drive. The work should be a love that stimulates the mind to always think, the body to laugh, and the spirit to be alive.

The third component is the right context or fit. The passion becomes more natural, and the person is more likely to be true to their "self," if a leader continues to ask the question of how to put oneself and those that follow their lead in the space that fits best with their skills.

An introverted colleague pointed me in the direction of that article after I was pushed to lead. For that, I am grateful.

18. Pierre Clements—Global National Accounts Leader/Entrepreneur:

Over my career, I have been blessed to work with several of the largest, most-recognized Fortune 500 companies in the world (Coca-Cola and Kraft Foods) and have also worked with some great leaders. For me, the most valuable lessons personally were learned and applied from my late father, Ernest Clements, a retired educator and principal of thirty-four years.

Specifically, at an early phase he would say to me, "You can't get ahead by laying in the bed." This framework translated into my personal beliefs of hard work, integrity, authenticity, and relationships in all aspects of my life. In order to make critical decisions, you must operate with the highest ethical standards as part of your decision tree, collaborate with all relevant stakeholders, complete a risk assessment of the desired outcome, and follow your instincts. This philosophy has allowed me to successfully negotiate over one billion dollars in customer contractual revenue over my business career.

19. Karin Hurt—Author, Consultant, MBA Professor, CEO, Let's Grow Leaders:

When I was a young communications graduate student at the University of Maryland, I met the best door opener of my career. I was working on a research project around empowering leadership. I noticed that nearly everyone I was reading was citing the same guy, Dr. Henry Sims. Since this was before the days you could Google answers in an instant, I went to the library and found one of his books, *SuperLeadership: Leading Others to Lead Themselves*.

I flipped to the back page to read about the authors. I had to laugh. Dr. Sims taught across campus at the business school. I read the book in one sitting, picked up the book and my recent writing, ran across campus, and knocked on his door. He stopped what he was doing, and we talked for several hours; he practiced everything he had written about. He led me to lead myself. He asked provocative questions and made me think. He challenged me to consider my direction—not just in my research but also in my career. I left my paper with him for comment.

When I came back the next week, he said, "I think I can help you publish this," which he did, and the next several hours of in-depth discussion led me to understand that what I really wanted to do was to be working in organizations, not studying them, and that what I needed most was not an academic advisor but a contact. Then he began opening doors. The next week he took me to lunch with a director doing leadership work in the company I have worked for ever since.

Hank has remained my mentor and my friend. When I get stuck, I knock. He always has questions, ideas, and contacts (mostly other folks for whom he's opened doors). I knocked just last month. I asked Hank why he opens doors for students and others. (Ironically, I never did take a class from him.)

In retrospect, the best part of my academic career has been the influence and support I have been able to provide to others. I have tried to act and behave as a "SuperLeader."

The benefit of knocking is that some SuperLeader may open a door. Knock. Answer. Lead.

PART 7
NOTES FROM THE AUTHOR

Beans Wall Quote #175: "The final test of a leader is that he leaves behind him in other men the conviction and the will to carry on." — Walter Lippmann

MY LEADERSHIP RESIDUE STORY:

At the start of my professional career, I worked with a leader who personified the marriage between strategy and execution. He expected even entry-level sales representatives to follow through on commitments at a high level (execution); and understand and be able to articulate *why* each task was necessary for the company's global success (strategy). His leadership linked our actions with the company's mission. He would frequently remind us, "We are constantly being evaluated. Those who succeed not only know the right answers, they know *why* they are right." This leader's name is Joe Cavaliere. We have both since changed companies, and I have not talked with Joe for decades. Still, with every new work project, I simultaneously consider strategy, execution, and the project's connection to a more global mission.

When I joined my next company, I came to know a senior leader who required his managers to take personal ownership of his or her assigned responsibility, as if we were the CEO for our portion of the company. He was extremely good at removing barriers as long as we were up-front about the true drivers of the business and specific about what we needed to move forward. His managers were allowed only one opportunity to blame poor business results on the weather, the economy, the decisions of a predecessor, or any other external force.

The first (and only) time a manager blamed a business failure on an external force, the senior leader would share "The Submarine Story": "A submarine captain docks his ship for the last time after twenty years of exemplary service and hands the keys to you. On your maiden voyage, you take the submarine out one hundred miles and crash into an iceberg. Who crashed the submarine?"

Of course, the new manager would say, "Well...I suppose...I would have been the one to crash the submarine."

The senior executive would then explain the moral of his story. "This business is your submarine now. It doesn't matter what happened under the previous captain's leadership or the forces that surround you. You have to own the results. Know what is driving your business and deliver the plan *anyway*."

This leader's name is Stan Hutchen. He retired in 2002. Stan's leadership has impacted me in small ways, such as his advice to "always wear a sport coat when presenting or attending a business meeting." He has impacted me in more significant ways as well. During every business results discussion since meeting Stan, I have thought about "The Submarine Story" and how he seized learning moments to develop his leaders for the long-term.

Examples of leadership from Joe and Stan have positive residue with me. Their memories influence my decisions weekly, sometimes impacting millions of dollars in revenue and hundreds of people who may never meet Joe or Stan. These two men ignited my passion for developing others, culminating in my writing the very book you are reading. Their leadership residue transcends time and formal reporting structures.

MY LEADERSHIP PLATFORM: BUILDING BRIDGES, SOLVING PROBLEMS, AND LEADING AUTHENTICALLY

I Am Passionate About:

Accelerating the performance of smart and courageous leaders who aspire to be even better. I envision a world where every leader embraces his or her responsibility to inspire greatness in others.

I Believe:
1. **Every major success or failure begins and ends with leadership.** Leaders are constantly watched and evaluated by their followers. Those who make a difference are purposeful about wanting to leave a positive residue for those who choose to follow.
2. **Attitude is contagious.** Pessimistic people can't help but ruin your day. Optimistic people would help you change the world. Your perspective is always a choice.
3. **Collaboration creates value.** Everyone needs help achieving goals. We are all better than well-intended clichés that only validate self-sufficiency, a pull-yourself-up-by-your-bootstraps mentality, the self-made man, the army of one, Rambo, and John Wayne. As the world grows more complex, the winners will be those who have authentic relationships allowing them to access information and resources.

4. **Transparency is more powerful than self-righteousness.** Honest humility is owning the reality of being human—strengths as well as shortcomings. False humility and unsupported arrogance serve no one.
5. **The right questions are more valuable than having all the right answers.** There is power in asking thoughtful questions. Effective leaders retain their childlike curiosity and are able to transfer their curiosity to others charged with solving problems.
6. **God has designed everyone to be the best in the world at *something*.** Fear holds us back from finding our *thing*. Some may fear the temporary discomfort and embarrassment of the learning process. Some may be afraid of the responsibility of being labeled a subject-matter expert. Others may be afraid of possible isolation from making others feel less than average. If unguarded, fear will seduce us into settling for good enough or to sabotage others rather than help others succeed. Find your *thing* and help others find theirs.

EPILOGUE: HERE'S THE POINT

My life and professional experiences have been like those of many others. I have suffered through managers whose titles and position power were their only levers for leading others. As their direct report, and even as a peer, these managers caused me to question the purpose of my existence and likelihood of contributing anything of value to the corporate mission. To hear their names in conversation, even today, leaves me feeling drained and conjures emotions of lacking. My emotions were validated every time these managers tried to *make* me do something, because...well...they were in charge, and the conversation was supposed to end there.

I have also had leaders inspire me to willingly invest personal resources to achieve goals that I believed to be far from probable. As a child might find courage in the dark with only a towel draped over his or her shoulders as a cape, these leaders caused me to feel confident and able to conquer any challenge. Just thinking of these leaders conjures supernatural inspiration to solve problems strategically and creatively. No coercion is required for me to work long hours, embracing projects and common goals as if my very existence depends on these leaders' success. And I am not alone.

In these pages, lawyers, business executives, ministers, and educators from every walk of life shared how they continue to be inspired by people in their pasts. More than a particular task or project, people attribute lessons learned from other leaders as being the defining determinants of successes. Nido R. Qubein—businessman, motivational speaker, and president of High Point University—defines an effective leader as "one who creates capacity in others." US president John Quincy Adams said, "If your actions inspire others to dream more, learn more, do more, and become more, you are a leader." I believe both are right. I bet you, like Dorothy, can think of someone in your past who continues to inspire you to be more.

This fable and collection of true leadership-residue stories highlight a distinction between management and leadership that is often missed. We can define management as getting people to complete specific tasks measurably better than they did previously. Leadership is about giving people the tools, capability, and freedom to fly to heights not previously considered against tasks or challenges not currently apparent. Where management is focused on reinforcing boundaries and guardrails needed to deliver budgets, leadership challenges people to think differently so they can knock down the barriers of business as usual.

Much like Dorothy in this fable, my passion for leadership grew out of my observations of how leaders around me influence success. Once I committed to improve my own effectiveness in leading others, my work began with honest self-discovery. My leadership platform guides how I negotiate people-management issues, office politics, and career choices that tempt me to stray from personal strengths and long-term aspirations. Without doing this work ahead of time, it would be easy to be lured by the emotion of a new job offering more money or an impressive title. Without a guidepost, an aspiring leader faces life currents as a leaf might attempt to navigate whitewater rapids. Anyone following this leader does not know what to expect. Without a premeditated platform, the leader him- or herself is left to make a difficult decision in the moment while balancing the stress and adrenaline often accompanying difficult decisions.

The hard truth remains: leaders are 100 percent accountable for the team's success. There is no all-knowing wizard behind the curtain. There is no cross-functional department head to blame. There is only the leader. It is true no one succeeds alone; however, the leader creates the environment in which teams operate. The leader establishes the picture of success, inspires action, and removes barriers that stand in the way. Success and failure are unmistakably tied to the leader's preparedness and performance in these three priorities.

Although leaders must be mindful of ensuring short term results, these results should not be at the sacrifice of the long-term capacities of others. If the leader continuously has to don a cape and fly in to save the day, leadership effectiveness is limited. Followers will never feel the need to develop what is needed to rescue themselves. When success is dependent on a promise of incentive or threat of punishment, leadership effectiveness is limited. Results are temporary at best. It is flawed to evaluate a leader's effectiveness based on monthly revenue performance or quarterly earnings. A measure of a leader's success must include his or her ability to inspire success even after he or she has gone. Is there influence that remains? Is there leadership residue?

I hope this book has helped you identify the type of legacy you would like to leave for others. You can join the global leadership conversation, access additional development tools, or leave your leadership-residue story at the following sites:

Facebook: https://www.facebook.com/LeadersResidue
Twitter: https://twitter.com/LeadersResidue
Blog: https://leadershipresidue.wordpress.com
Website: www.Leadership-Residue.com

Beans Wall Quote #191: "The master in the art of living makes little distinction between his work and his play, his labor and his leisure, his mind and his body, his education and his recreation, his love and his religion. He hardly knows which is which. He simply pursues his vision of excellence at whatever he does, leaving others to decide whether he is working or playing. To him he is always doing both." — James Michener

Made in the USA
Middletown, DE
04 February 2016